Conversation with the Prince

Tadeusz Różewicz

Conversation with the Prince

AND OTHER POEMS

introduced and translated
by Adam Czerniawski

Anvil Press Poetry

Published in 1982
by Anvil Press Poetry Ltd
69 King George Street London SE10 8PX
85646 079 6
Distributed by Wildwood House Ltd

This book is published
with financial assistance from
The Arts Council of Great Britain

Printed in Great Britain at
The Camelot Press Ltd, Southampton

Contents

from *Regio* (1969)

from *A Traumatic Tale* (1979)

Introduction

I

Born in 1921, Tadeusz Różewicz belongs to the generation whose formal education was abruptly terminated in 1939. In fact, Różewicz himself left school in 1938 because his father, a minor official, could not afford to keep him there. By then Różewicz had already published his first poems in a school magazine.

Some of his generation of poets, like Baczyński, Gajcy and Stroiński, died in the Warsaw Rising; others, like Borowski, went to prison or concentration camps, while Herbert and Białoszewski remained unpublished long after the war because of censorship.

Różewicz's own experience of the war was also typical: odd menial jobs to keep alive, graduation from a clandestine military school, participation in the Resistance, publication from a makeshift secret press. When the occupation ended, he was able to write:

> I am twenty-four
> led to slaughter
> I survived

He entered Kraków University to study art history and in 1947 published *Niepokój (Anxiety)*, his first volume of poetry.

It was no accident that I chose to study history of art. I did it in order to rebuild the Gothic temple, to raise inside myself that church brick by brick, in order to reconstruct man bit by bit [. . .]. I was full of reverential wonder at works of art (the aesthetic experience replaced religious experience) but simultaneously I felt a growing contempt for all 'aesthetic' values. I felt that something had come to an end for ever for me and for humanity. Too early I came to understand Mickiewicz's dictum that 'it is more difficult to spend a day well than to write a book' [. . .]. So I tried to rebuild what seemed to me most important for life and for the life of poetry: ethics. And because from my earliest youth I associated politics with ethics rather than aesthetics, my work had a political tinge, and 'political' for me meant socially progressive [. . .]. That is why, despite my attentive apprenticeship with the masters of the word, I never took any interest in the so-called

11

poetic schools and their market-place biddings concerning versification and metaphor.[1]

In 1966 Różewicz received the highest Polish literary award: the State Prize for Literature, Class I. In 1971 a representative sample of the youngest Polish poets voted him the most important living Polish poet. Różewicz has travelled widely in the East and West as far as China and the United States, reading his poetry to audiences familiar with his work through many translations. His experimental plays have also been successfully performed in Poland and abroad.

II

Poets reveal themselves through what they say about other poets. Różewicz has compiled imaginative selections of the poetry of Leopold Staff, who died in 1957, and of Józef Czechowicz, killed in a German air-raid in 1939.

Throughout his long career—his first book appeared in 1901—Staff held the admiration of the public and of the critics, but his poetry was decidedly traditional in form and represented the broad Parnassian and neo-classical stream in Polish pre-war poetry. Różewicz characterized this poetry as 'Ham acting. The illness of literature. The greatest illness of poetry [. . .] which linked the poetry of "Young Poland" and "Skamander". Abuse of the word is a feature common to all these poets.'[2] Why, then, is Różewicz taking an interest in this hamming? The answer lies in 'Awakening', one of Staff's post-war poems which Różewicz quotes in his commentary:

> It's dawn,
> But there is no light.
> I am half-awake,
> A mess all round.
> I ought to tie up this,
> Connect that
> And reach a decision.

[1] Tadeusz Różewicz, *Przygotowanie do wieczoru autorskiego*, Warsaw 1971, pp. 89–91.
[2] Różewicz's 'Postface' to Staff's *Kto jest ten dziwny nieznajomy?*, Warsaw 1976, p. 192.

I know nothing.
I can't find my shoes,
I can't find myself.
I have a headache.

Różewicz then explains:

The dance of poetry came to an end during the Second World War in concentration camps created by totalitarian systems [. . .]. The departure in such *Grenzsituationen* [the term is Karl Jaspers' whom Różewicz also quotes—A. Cz.] from the special 'poetic' language has produced those poems which I call stripped of masks and costumes. Our critics talked of the 'prosaicization' of poetry. This was a simplified and mistaken view. It is precisely the poems written in *Grenzsituationen*, in ultimate situations, 'prosaicized' works, which created the conditions for poetry's subsistence and even survival. In the works of every writer, even the greatest, such poems are very rare [. . .]. Of course, there are poets who perform their 'poetry dance' resolutely to the end without reference to the state of humanity, their country or even their own condition.[3]

Różewicz concludes that Staff's poetry had progressed 'from "The Blacksmith", the unblemished perfect sonnet, to "Awakening", which is not a poem, but rather a description of a situation the poet had found himself in; it is a piece of information passed by the poet to other people, it is a work which one might also call a poem . . .'.[3]

Not all inter-war Polish poetry was Parnassian and neo-classical. There were several powerful modernist movements rich both in creative and theoretical achievements. But one of the innovators, Czechowicz, stood apart from the battles of manifestoes and excommunications, even though he had acquired a large following and was dubbed 'Prince of the Poets'. Of him Różewicz writes:

Czechowicz wasn't a metropolitan poet, he wasn't a tribune, he was not a political or a court poet [. . .]. Czechowicz almost never raises his voice, one could say he shouts his drama in a whisper [. . .]. Czechowicz is a poet of the provinces and he always remained a part of the provinces, although he ceased being a provincial poet [. . .]. Many poets who inhabit the capital remain typical provincial poets to the end.[4]

These comments come from a poet who was born in sleepy Radomsko,

---

[3] Op. cit., pp. 194–5.
[4] From Różewicz's 'Preface' to Czechowicz's *Wybór wierszy*, Warsaw 1967, p. 6.

spent the war years in the forests, then settled for some twenty years in remote Gliwice, has since moved to Wrocław and is rarely seen in Warsaw. They come from the author of 'Conversation with the Prince' and are addressed to the first Polish translator of T. S. Eliot. Różewicz had an elder brother Janusz (also a member of the Resistance, executed by the Gestapo in 1944) who corresponded with Czechowicz and had sent him his first poems for comment. Two of Czechowicz's replies have survived. In one of them, dated 4 December 1937, Czechowicz writes:

Dear Sir,
The last two poems you've sent me I admire much less [. . .]. All the same, I would very much like you to surpass Czechowicz, for as far as my own worries go, my concern regarding the 'royal succession' is paramount. I have many imitators, too many—in Warsaw there is talk of a 'Czechowicz School'—but, alas, they detract from my achievement. I have not come across anyone who is a continuer of my line rather than an epigone or a *pasticheur*.[5]

Czechowicz's lean and controlled yet free-flowing and fluid poetry breaks with traditional moulds. Its muted music and imagery uncannily express the foreboding of the storm that was to engulf him in 1939. Różewicz, writing at the end of the storm, assembles his own poetic on the ground cleared by Czechowicz in order to confront the *Grenzsituation* the older poet had not survived to experience. To call the result 'poetry' may, as we have already seen from Różewicz's comment on Staff's 'Awakening', sound paradoxical. But then what can Różewicz mean by his claim that he is 'not a poet'?[6] Two separate but related issues are involved.

As we saw, Różewicz's respect for Staff arose from the fact that Staff succeeded in freeing himself from the rhetorical posturing of his pre-war verse. It might perhaps be argued that it was the war and the occupation which forced Staff, as it did Różewicz, to devise a suitably austere style to cope with horrors of such magnitude. (I think it is safe to assume that Różewicz would have approved of such a development whatever the political and social circumstances in which it was being effected.) However, what is significant about Staff is that during and after the war his poetry remained almost totally aloof from contemporary events.

[5] Józef Czechowicz, *Listy*, Lublin 1977, pp. 382–3.
[6] Tadeusz Różewicz, *Przygotowanie do wieczoru autorskiego*, p. 189.

This, of course, was not Różewicz's way, and thus we see in his poetry the merging of two reasons supportive of a preference for poetry shorn of all traditional prettifying devices: his fundamental distaste for rhetoric, coupled with the urgent task of finding a language that would adequately bear witness to a world emerging from the trauma of World War II.

III

Because of its precarious history, Poland's writers had always recognized their duty to reflect the *Grenzsituationen* of a nation in perpetual crisis. But while the great nineteenth-century poets—Mickiewicz, Słowacki, Norwid—found suitable objective correlatives in their poetry and drama, catastrophic events, like wholesale deportations and killings in Soviet and German camps, tended to elicit from writers barely articulate screams of anguish and indignation, though there were some exceptions. For example, Tadeusz Borowski's concentration-camp stories succeed because the author hit on the device of treating the grossly abnormal as absolutely normal: in one typical story the number gassed during a single round is related to the goals scored in a football game between teams of camp guards. But even Borowski failed to devise a parallel schema for his poetry which remained shackled in traditional forms. To an extent this is also true of Miłosz's war-time poetry. While he, like Różewicz, denounced the beauties of verse, proclaimed the superiority of ethics over aesthetics and composed his 'Naive Poems', his poetry retained strong formal links with neo-classicism and has a firmly traditional diction. Only Różewicz succeeded in forging a poetry to which the epithet 'anti-poetry' could legitimately be applied and which could therefore bear the weight of the events it described.

It was this moral preoccupation, this concern with truth rather than beauty, with the telling particular rather than the platitudinous abstraction, that enabled Różewicz to record with dignity and passionate humanity the incomprehensible terror of those days. The poignance of, say, 'Pigtail' or of 'Massacre of the Boys' is effortlessly created out of a laconic, matter-of-fact account of its exhibits. This principally dark vision continues to be reflected even in his most recent poetry. But now it is concentrated less on the specific horrors of the past, more often it voices a general despair at the follies of mankind and a half-resigned acceptance of mortality.

15

In the mid-fifties—when Różewicz was writing the halting, spare 'In the Midst of Life'—Gombrowicz published his characteristically provocative and abrasive essay 'Against Poets'. In it he attacked and ridiculed the 'excess of poetry, excess of poetical words, excess of metaphor, excess of sublimation, excess of condensation and the elimination of all anti-poetic elements . . .'.[7] If Gombrowicz's diatribe strikes us as anachronistic and beside the point, this is an indication of how profound a revolution Różewicz has effected.

A major consequence of Różewicz's directness and lack of self-consciousness is that his art is non-selective, curiously impartial. There are no special themes; he has no axes to grind. Różewicz does not choose subjects because they happen to fit his views on art, politics, man, religion, the plight of the poor, or whatever. Anything he has experienced can, and does, get transmuted into poetry. Perhaps the most impressive poems are those in which he picks on some very ordinary object—a bird-cage in 'Laughter', a piece of rope in 'The End', grass growing in the crevice of a wall in 'Grass', a newspaper in 'he tears easily . . .'—and uses it as a powerful, ramified metaphor, without any appearance of forced ingenuity. As he says,

I tend to find any old newspaper more absorbing than the finest edition of poems. Hence my sudden revulsion against Rilke. My motto was Norwid's 'A proper word to name each thing'. I was aiming at a poetry of absolute transparency, so that the dramatic material might be seen through the poem, just as in clear water you can see what is moving on the bottom. And so the form had to vanish, had to become transparent, it had to become identified with the subject of the given poem.[8]

But precisely because Różewicz is a permanently contemporary poet, living always in the present, his delight in ordinary human existence allowed him to overcome despair and regain faith in poetry. Perhaps this is why he is such a prolific and popular writer. The second edition of his collected poems runs to over 700 pages.

This also explains why Różewicz writes so many poems about poetry. For him, deliberation on this subject is not confined to announcing an artistic programme, pontificating on the role of the artist in society or

[7] Witold Gombrowicz, *Dziennik 1953–1956*, Paris 1957, p. 317.

[8] 'Tadeusz Różewicz in Conversation with Adam Czerniawski', *The New Review* No. 25, London 1976, p. 10.

bewailing the loss of inspiration. Because he is committed to turning into poetry a whole range of experience, from the most trivial to the most profound, it follows that, for him, poetry-writing is neither a pastime nor a profession, but a way of life. So the nature and purpose of poetry have to be constantly scrutinized and questioned. Hence also the passion, the urgency, the sarcasm and the barely controlled, pulsating violence in so many of his poems: the image of a tiger in 'Feeding Time', of a slaughter-house in 'At the Same Time', or a sheep's heart being pulled out of its warm body in 'To the Heart'. The poems themselves are like wild beasts in 'Forms' or, in 'Birth of a New Poem', they flow 'through the foetal waters of humanity'.

The juxtaposition of animal behaviour with human and divine passions serves simultaneously to diminish and to enhance animal, man and god. The king of the beasts is shown in an undignified posture in 'Feeding Time'; 'The New Man' is like a sewage pipe, while Christ crawls on all fours like a dog in 'Wood' and is apologetic about the miracles in 'Unrecorded Epistle'. In 'Leda' it is the girl who emerges triumphant, while Zeus is wrenched away from her, bleeding.

Since Różewicz has travelled extensively, it is natural for him to make full use of a wide range of cultural references. But he never employs such material in the manner of Yeats, Stevens, Pound, Eliot or Norwid; that is, he does not use it to create a paradigm of an idealized civilization. He does not single out cultural objects and events for special reverential treatment as touchstones of value. In Paris or Milan the poet is as aware of whores at railway stations as he is of paintings in galleries, and he makes no effort to demonstrate as Norwid, Pound or Eliot would have done that the lofty is preferable to the sordid.

Similarly, when Różewicz alludes to historical events or monuments— say, the Wall of China in 'A Lesson in Patience'—or to a literary classic— *Hamlet* in 'Précis'—the purpose is not to celebrate them, but to show how they impinge on a modern consciousness. It is no accident that we are given the precise date when the poet's son 'learnt of the English dramatist's existence'. The poem opens with a summary of the plot, but the emphasis is not on the Shakespeare play but on its possible effect on the mind of his teenage son and on the significance for our time of Hamlet's famous question. The *fin de siècle* world finds a place in 'Kazimierz Przerwa-Tetmajer' not because Różewicz wants to proclaim some theory about the relevance to us of late nineteenth-century literature and art, but because Tetmajer, the once immensely popular author of sensuous

17

and languorous sonnets composed in the 1890s, died forgotten in a gutter in the German-occupied Warsaw of Różewicz's youth.

It is in keeping with the practice I am claiming for Różewicz that the 'I' of the poems—and most of them are written in the first person—appears to be genuinely autobiographical, not an invented persona. Thus, when Różewicz writes about natural beauty in 'Golden Mountains', he concentrates on the difficulty of communicating his experience to another person. It matters more to the young poet to share his excitement than to imbue it with mysticism, pantheism or any vague unfocused emotion. At the same time, by ignoring the aesthetic and the contemplative, Różewicz qualitatively equates this excitement with any other 'ordinary' happening.

In his fascinating study (in *Meaning in the Visual Arts*) of the inscription 'Et in Arcadia Ego' as it appears in Poussin's two paintings, Erwin Panofsky shows the ambiguity of the phrase: there is some reason to regard the 'Ego' as referring, in one of the paintings, to the dead shepherd on whose tomb the legend appears, but there is also reason to see this as a reference to death present even in the blissful realm of Arcady. Later Goethe gave the phrase an ecstatic rather than a melancholy significance when he prefaced his *Italienische Reise* with the exclamation 'Auch ich in Arkadien!' The visual and the literary interpretations merge in Różewicz's 'Et in Arcadia Ego', one of his most ambitious works. Here the subject of the reference is (i) death, (ii) the barbarian visitor from the North, (iii) the poet himself, and (iv) that same barbarian poet in the role of an exiled rather than dead shepherd who—see the closing line of the poem—dwelt in Arcady for a while.

This complexity of reference enables Różewicz to create a richly-textured model capable of containing the contradictions of beauty, destruction and death. In the end he rejects the seductive charms of Italian art, landscape and history because he bears witness to facts of such power that when confronted with them, these riches pale into insignificance. In 1946 Różewicz wrote the poem 'Mask' and an extract from it appears in 'Et in Arcadia Ego'. The poet hints that the dweller of a distant northerly land for whom, as Goethe reports, the Italian has nothing but contempt, has knowledge of which the Arcadian shepherd is totally unaware. For he comes from a land where the archaeological digs are not of sculpted masterpieces:

> objects excavated in my country have small black
> heads sealed with plaster and horrible grins.

18

As he confesses in the final line of the poem, he had 'tried to return to paradise' but that attempt had to fail.

Like most Poles, Różewicz has his roots in Roman Catholicism and for him, as for many of them, the Church is not so much a moral and intellectual force, as a presence felt at all levels of Polish culture and consciousness. Różewicz recalls:

As far as I can remember, my first poem was called 'The Wooden Church' and it appeared in 1938. Later, I was tearing myself away not only from customary beliefs and the liturgy, but also from the umbilical cord which tied me to heaven. But of course the seeds of childhood remained: the devil, angels, the good Lord.[9]

There are many poems in which Różewicz makes powerful use of Christian mythology, his attitude being that of a sympathetic sceptic who has experienced the tradition from the inside. In 'Thorn', the dramatically expressed protestations of disbelief are subtly combined with the poet's conviction that, when stripped of theological and dogmatic accretions, the Christian myth is revealed as rooted in vital human experience. 'The Return', 'Wood' and 'Death' build upon homely images of faith, while 'Unrecorded Epistle' depicts its exasperating fickleness.

The main strength of Różewicz's craft comes from an extremely skilful blending of two seemingly irreconcilable elements: a rich sensuality restrained by a frugal language. Does this come through in translation? Perhaps English is particularly well suited to Różewicz's poetry, for Polish reviewers have said that he sometimes sounds better in English than in Polish. But even if it is true that he sounds *as good*, the problem of presenting him to an English-speaking readership does not end there. Every English-language poet creates in the tradition of his native tongue and its literature, passionately taking up some strands of that tradition, scornfully rejecting others. Clearly, a foreign poet, especially one like Różewicz, who neither speaks nor reads English, cannot be fitted into such a pattern. A translator may, however, detect distinct affinities with particular poets writing in English and try to bring them out either in translation or, obliquely, in a commentary. In the case of Różewicz I see no obvious affinities, though very occasionally a telling comparison may be found. There is a short lyric by Emily Dickinson which reads:

[9] Op. cit., p. 11.

Water, is taught by thirst.
Land—by the Oceans passed.
Transport—by throe—
Peace—by its battles told—
Love, by Memorial Mold—
Birds, by snow.

The juxtaposition of sensuality and austerity, a feature as strong in Dickinson as it is in Różewicz, is here pressed to its limits. Różewicz's 'Draft for a Contemporary Love Poem' reads like a slightly elaborated version of Emily Dickinson's poem. What the translator needs to do is, on the one hand, to resist the temptation to 'poeticize' Różewicz's diction (for such poeticization would amount to the most blatant betrayal of the originals); but on the other hand, he must not be misled by its simplicity. Różewicz's poems are very carefully constructed and their balance is easily upset by awkward, pedestrian syntax and language which creates an impression of shoddy vulgarity.

IV

A grey wet late afternoon in a Kraków bookshop. A group of young people come in, demanding Różewicz's *Collected Poems*. Not a hope. The first edition of 5,000 had sold out, now the second edition of 10,000 is also gone.

At our meeting in Kraków in 1979 Różewicz says, 'We were watching the Pope on the telly addressing his millions in Warsaw and my son said to me, "Dad, you've no chance of ever pulling in a crowd like that."'

Artists have to be insufferably megalomaniac. This is their protective armour against frustration and disappointment. They have to wear it even when, like Różewicz, they become established and internationally celebrated. Fame is a relative evaluation which is constantly outstripped by ambition. But there are ways of being self-absorbed. Różewicz wears his ambition to rule the souls of men lightly. Over the years of friendship I see an unostentatious man radiating warmth and good humour.

So, as I come to the conclusion of the Introduction to my third selection of his poetry, I am reluctant to dwell exclusively on the achievement of a sombre witness to ghastly truths and would like to hint at the bright side of Różewicz the man, normally carefully hidden from his readers. Thus I think of him pretending to be a petrified saint in the ruined nave of Tintern Abbey, of the time when we had to share a creaky double bed in a friend's disfurnished flat in Amsterdam and he said, 'Let's call the Press—this will cause a sensation!', I think of his acquiring a taste for fresh salmon and thereafter pestering bewildered English barmaids for 'So-loh-mohn' sandwiches. I also remember him patiently sitting through a puppet show at a primary school open day and declaring the piece too avant-garde to follow.

When Różewicz attended the 1977 Cambridge Poetry Festival we went to see an exhibition of Blake's works and memorabilia. He took off his spectacles and placed them with an impish grin on top of a show-case containing Blake's curiously framed glasses. This was an uncanny spontaneous recreation of the theme of 'Cage 1974': the life and death of a poet, his relationship with people, the smart strictures of professional critics, the mindlessly adulatory posthumous fame. Suddenly, there was a moment at which Różewicz's boyish clowning turns into serious-minded poetry.

V

The present selection is broadly representative of Różewicz's total output in that it shows the early contrasting preoccupations with love and war, the uncertain role of the poet in the modern world, reactions to contemporary events ranging from the grotesquely farcical to the grotesquely sensual, and, in the most recent work, a poetry luminously elegiac, ruminative and intensely personal in its combination of serenity, resignation and resolute strength. But on the relationship between it and its readers, let Różewicz have the last word:

I search books and poems for practical help. I hope they will help me overcome despair and doubt and, strangely enough, I sought help both in Dostoevsky and in Conrad. Similarly, I sought help during the Occupation, and even before, in poetry. And when this led to disappointment—after all, these were only books—I became angry and disillusioned with the greatest works. I felt I was muddling things up in some way and yet I couldn't face up to this. Because I myself have always searched, begged for help, I began to think that I too may be able to help, though of course I also have moments when I feel it's not worth anything. Occasionally, someone writes to me in a way that strengthens my conviction regarding my determination to turn words into practice.[10]

ADAM CZERNIAWSKI
London, July 1981

[10] Op. cit., p. 16.

Translator's Note

The present edition reproduces most of the poems published in *Faces of Anxiety* (Rapp & Whiting, London, 1969) and in *Selected Poems* (Penguin Books, 1976), both now out of print. It includes previously uncollected and newer translations some of which have appeared in *Ambit*, *Encounter*, *Poetry Nation*, *Stand*, *The New Review* and a BBC Radio 3 programme of Różewicz's poetry entitled 'The Dead Have Remembered'.

The translations are based on the second edition of *Poezje zebrane* (Wrocław, 1976), but with some authorial corrections, *Opowiadanie traumatyczne* (Kraków, 1979) and a few recent unpublished texts.

It is twenty years since I published my first Różewicz translations. If they have improved with time, my wife Ann must be given due credit.

Conversation with the Prince

Cage 1974

Birds flying
through this room
turn into silence

poems
become objects
dark physical literal
you can tie them round your neck

Here I'm visited
by my double
my alter ego
der Doppelgänger

he derides me
in my shabby coat-poem
he laughs convulsively
it's the one—I conclude—they say
screams just like me but in moderation
relieves himself
like me
but with more refinement
weeps like me but more beautifully

people who pass
through this room drop their voices
stealthily touch the furniture
the spines of books I've read
they stare at the pen the comb
the spectacles
the now mystic body
of the faithful life-companion
at a manuscript of an unfinished
poem

I was giving birth to a devil
in the desert
he was dragging along the sand
I was giving birth to him with my anus
he was crawling out of non-being
out of me
the moaning core
yellowish-black glistening
heavy insipid
covered in mucus
he was turning into
a blood-shot eye

a body leaving my
body
leaving me
evacuating me
changing me
into nothing
into a black hole

waspish critics who pass
through this room
read the manuscript
of the unfinished
poem
with distaste

that artificial pathos
that excrement
that bile blood water
that exhibitionism
they shrug their shoulders
and leave the workroom
of a poet who took
his

1974

Mask

I watch a film about a Venetian carnival
huge effigies with monstrous heads
laugh noiselessly from ear to ear
and a maid too beautiful for me
an inhabitant of a small town in the North
rides astride an ichthyosaurus.

Objects excavated in my country have small black
heads sealed with plaster and horrible grins
but we too have a motley roundabout
and a girl in black tights decoys
an elephant and two blue lions with raspberry tongues
and catches a wedding ring in flight.

Our recalcitrant bodies reluctant to mourn,
the roofs of our mouths savour a dessert,
go adjust paper streamers and garlands
lean over like this: let hip touch hip
your thighs are alive
let's run away, let's run.

1946

Mother of Hanged Men

She rubs against the crowd's rough skin.

Here
the mother of hanged men
walks
through the street
black
she carries a silver head
in her hands
oh what a heavy lump
filled with darkness
shattered with light

out of her mind she circles
and sings and sings
her shoes have broken heels
her womb is barren
her breasts dry
a siren out of her mind she howls
to the swollen moon above the roofs

with leaden feet she paces
the concrete streets
the mother of the hanged,
the moon round her neck,
sinks to the bottom
rubs against the crowd's rough scales.

Two Judgements

I see
the smile
removed from his white face
against the wall.

The Stranger the harbinger of death
bowed his head
lower.

By the stove
I see
a funny statue of pain
in well-trodden slippers
a tiny crooked
little figure
of a petrified mother.

The Survivor

I am twenty-four
led to slaughter
I survived.

The following are empty synonyms:
man and beast
love and hate
friend and foe
darkness and light.

The way of killing men and beasts is the same
I've seen it:
truckfuls of chopped-up men
who will not be saved.

Ideas are mere words:
virtue and crime
truth and lies
beauty and ugliness
courage and cowardice.

Virtue and crime weigh the same
I've seen it:
in a man who was both
criminal and virtuous.

I seek a teacher and a master
may he restore my sight hearing and speech
may he again name objects and ideas
may he separate darkness from light.

I am twenty-four
led to slaughter
I survived.

Purification

Don't be ashamed of tears
don't be ashamed of tears young poets.

Marvel at the moon
the moonlit night
marvel at pure love and the nightingale's song.

Fear not ascension into heaven
reach for the star
compare eyes to stars.

Be moved by a primrose
an orange butterfly
by the rising and the setting sun.

Feed gentle pigeons
observe with a smile
dogs engines flowers and rhinos.

Talk about ideals
recite an ode to youth
trust a passing stranger.

Naïve you will come to believe in beauty
moved you will come to believe in man.

Don't be ashamed of tears
don't be ashamed of tears young poets.

Living Star

What days entwine me
soft and perfumed
like beards of Assyrian merchants
so many days so many days
finely clustered

what nights swallow me
as dark as the gullet
wrapped in a red mucous membrane
so many nights so many nights
in the belly of a whale

My friend came
a hole in his forehead
and tore away fine beards
he tore apart the belly of delight
he ripped out
the limp spine of a reptile
and injected a new white marrow
like a star of quicksilver.

I See Madmen

I see madmen who
had walked on the sea
believing to the end
and went to the bottom

they still rock
my uncertain boat

cruelly alive I push away
those stiff hands

I push them away year after year.

A Visit

I couldn't recognize her
when I came in here
just as well it's possible
to take so long arranging these flowers
in this clumsy vase

'Don't look at me like that'
she said
I stroke the cropped hair
with my rough hand
'they cut my hair' she says
'look what they've done to me'

now again that sky-blue spring
begins to pulsate beneath the transparent
skin of her neck as always
when she swallows tears

why does she stare like that
I think well I must go
I say a little too loudly

and I leave her,
a lump in my throat

Chestnut

Saddest of all is leaving
home on an autumn morning
when there is no hope of an early return

The chestnut father planted in front
of the house grows in our eyes

mother is tiny
you could carry her in your arms

On the shelf
jars full of preserves
like sweet-lipped goddesses
have retained the flavour
of eternal youth

soldiers at the back of the drawer
will stay leaden till the end of the world

while God almighty who mixed in
bitterness with the sweetness
hangs on the wall helpless
and badly painted

childhood is like the worn face
on a golden coin that rings
true.

1947–48

The Return

Suddenly the window will open
and mother will call
it's time to come in

the wall will part
I will enter heaven in muddy shoes

I will come to the table
and answer questions rudely

I am all right leave me
alone. Head in hand I
sit and sit. How can I tell them
about that long
and tangled way.

Here in heaven mothers
knit green scarves

flies buzz

father dozes by the stove
after six days' labour.

No—surely I can't tell them
that men are at each
other's throats.

Mound

They heaped over him a mound
of arrivals and departures
of space and time
of men objects events
butter coffee newspapers
of plush green albums
bromide flowers
and artificial laughter

Almost everyone came
a copper leaf lies on the table
here they're scattering ash

The mother digs up the mound
and pulls out the young head
moulded in light
with a wide mouth
smelling of tobacco.

It's the One
whom you don't run to greet
outside the house
who isn't snoozing amid the raspberries
who won't be arriving tomorrow

The mother buried alive
in the air at table
moves her fingers
sluggishly

They

The weekday is beautiful
it begins with a crack of white

lips that are opposite and bitter
devour the dregs of night and sleep

faces strange and blind like puppies
open their eyes open their eyes

from each other's lips they pick
smiles and wonder

they feed each other
upon tongues of birds

when they perceive the obvious
they stifle a cry
ah! the sun the flower the breast

and the grey weekday morning
turns for them into wonder
like a blue elephant.

A Shell

Counting the money—is there enough
for a return home
(while at home the clatter of plates
and voices creaking
and water in a bucket
the colour of gall-stones
a change of shirt on Saturday
on Sunday a pudding and visitors
teenagers with knobbly knees)
the season's over
it's less expensive it's raining
I walk along the beach
passing the hulks of deserted cabins

The sea is vast

I can understand people
who flogged waves

I spent the last night
on a chair at a table
a harsh and lonely exile
swayed between
the sea and night-white
thighs of a girl
who only brought the tea

I sought help
I whispered into a pink shell
that I didn't want to go back
I begged and beseeched.

Abattoirs

Pink quartered ideals
hang in abattoirs

Shops are selling
clowns'
motley death-masks
stripped off the faces
of us who live
who have survived
staring
into the eye-socket of war.

But Whoever Sees . . .

But whoever sees my mother
in a purple smock in a white hospital
trembling
stiffening
with a wooden smile
and white gums

who for fifty years had faith
but now weeps and says
'I don't know . . . I don't know'

her face is like a large smudged tear
she clasps her hands like a frightened
little girl
her lips are blue

but whoever sees my mother
a hounded little animal
with a bulging eye

he

oh I would like to bear her upon my heart
and nourish her with sweetness

1947–48

41

What Luck

What luck I can pick
berries in the wood
I thought
there is no wood no berries.

What luck I can lie
in the shade of a tree
I thought trees
no longer give shade.

What luck I am with you
my heart beats so
I thought man
has no heart.

Pigtail

When all the women in the transport
had their heads shaved
four workmen with brooms made of birch twigs
swept up
and gathered up the hair

Behind clean glass
the stiff hair lies
of those suffocated in gas chambers
there are pins and side combs
in this hair

The hair is not shot through with light
is not parted by the breeze
is not touched by any hand
or rain or lips

In huge chests
clouds of dry hair
of those suffocated
and a faded plait
a pigtail with a ribbon
pulled at school
by naughty boys.

The Museum, Auschwitz, 1948

Massacre of the Boys

The children cried 'Mummy!
But I have been good!
It's dark in here! Dark!'

See them They are going to the bottom
See the small feet
they went to the bottom Do you see
that print
of a small foot here and there

pockets bulging
with string and stones
and little horses made of wire

A great closed plain
like a figure of geometry
and a tree of black smoke
a vertical
dead tree
with no star in its crown.

The Museum, Auschwitz, 1948

New Sun

I hear scraping
It's that old girl scratching
on the wall with her tiny claws
and coughing like a little animal

So I go to her
I sit at a round table
while she summons ghosts
out of a saucer and drinks tea
in small birdlike sips

On the what-not gentlemen
with beards
'jenseits von Gut und Böse'*
the last quarter of the 19th century

She shakes her dry little head
and talks about Venice
Florence and the Italian sun

I was born a baroness
This is the end of the world
now they've invented new suns and stars
—she says—
and her eyes fill with tears.

* beyond good and evil

Head in a Void

If you think you are
a beautiful head
set up
on high

if you think you are
the quick head
of a motionless trunk
which sinks in earth
blood and cow-dung

If you think you circle
upon pure orbits of the intellect
where from below you can hear only
the grunting bustling
and lip-smacking mob

if you think this
you are a head
which sways gently
in depopulated air

you are a head
which will be taken down
and cast aside.

Evocation of Childhood

In the light of day
he was happy as a bird
between bright swords of the sun
streaked with blood

A yellow kite gleamed
in the rolling smoke
like a dragon's eye

The boy believed he was a bird
he ran through green meadows
shouting

At night I am pursued
by his rapid breathing

The table on which I rest my head
is like the bole
of a felled tree

Witness

My dear, you know I am in
but don't suddenly enter
my room

You might see me
silent
over a blank sheet

Can you write
about love
when you hear the cries of
the slaughtered and disgraced
can you write
about death
watching the little faces
of children

Do not suddenly
enter my room

You will see
a dumb and bound
witness to love
overcome by death

1951–52

An Old Peasant Woman Walks
Along the Beach

She walks along the beach
in a clean white scarf

the wave runs towards her
young and chirrupy like the meadow
through which she rushed
to meet it

The old peasant woman walks
along the beach

She is still weary
and trembling
she is still full of the bustle
of the journey
of artificial lights
excited gestures
smoke over tables
of a stuffy night
in a closed compartment
the cold calling of loudspeakers
along vibrating platforms

She arrived here at dawn

Unknown flowers shivered
upon silver dunes
in sharp grasses
and pink lights

She walks
pressing a footmark on the sand
The first

woman from that village in the foothills
walks along the beach

the wave carries away the print
leaving
on the sand
a shell
with a light interior
of sea spices
rotting stems
extinguished
drops of amber
She walks
along the beach
bends over
scoops a handful of water
plunges her face in
feels the sea on her lips
like a tear

    *

In a white scarf
tied under her chin
her shoes slung over her shoulder
—that's the way she goes to market in the town
to save the soles—
she walks

For so many years she's been walking
through earth and water
through clods and hail
through rain and shine
stones and grass
through clouds and earth
through gates with shields
through stony churches

for half a century she's been walking

to the vast sea
until the new
workers' and peasants' rule
has brought her to the shore

The sea enters the sky
in the sky-sea
a gull screams
a white sea-crow
a tiny cradle on the crest

The old peasant woman
walks along the beach
picks a shell
listens
smiles
to the sky to the sea
to herself

Just such a shell lay
on the chest of drawers
among papier-mâché flowers
between pictures of saints
and a crystal ball
in which blue snow
fell eternally
the old folk said
the sea is enclosed in the shell
and the children's eyes sparkled

*

The young who were throwing and catching
a red ball across the roaring waves
saw an old woman
with a white scarf on her head

Her eyes half-closed
her face

gleamed in the light
like a flower after rain

The vast sea spoke

1952

The Colour of Her Eyes and Questions

Has my love
deep-blue eyes
with a silver speck
No

Does my dear
have hazel eyes
with a golden spark
No

Does my love
have black eyes
without light
No

My dear has eyes
which fall on me
like grey
autumnal rain

1954

Warmth

Since it's so cold
in the world
that men stare
so coldly
even
one's own children

you might as well
use a pot full of hot coffee
to warm your hands

the moment they wake
they speak in accents of tin and rust
they buzz and hiss

A Tree

Happy were
the poets of old
the world like a tree
they like a child

What shall I hang
upon the branch of a tree
which has suffered
a rain of steel

Happy were
the poets of old
around the tree
they danced like a child

What shall I hang
upon the branch of a tree
which is burnt
and never will sing

Happy were
the poets of old
beneath the oak
they sang like a child

But our tree
creaked in the night
with the weight
of a corpse despised

My Lips

This day is ending
It ends with supper
brushing of teeth
a kiss
and putting things in order

so it was a day
among those most precious days
which never return

What did happen to me

It passed and went
from morning till night
like the one before

Oh my day
the one and only
what have I done
what have I done

Yet perhaps one ought
to leave in the morning
return in the afternoon
repeat a few gestures
arrange many things

Oh my day
the most beautiful diamond in the world
house of gold
blue whale
the tear in my eyes

Oh my confused thoughts
when I stand hands in pockets

and watch through grey rods of rain
the maple-tree turn gold

My lips
which spoke
the truth lied
spoke by rote asserted
denied begged
screamed whispered
wept and laughed

My lips
shaping themselves
round countless
spoken words

1954–55

Love 1944

Naked defenceless
lips upon lips
eyes
wide open

listening

we drifted
across a sea
of tears and blood

1954

Who's Absent

To the memory of Zbyszek my little pupil

Who is drowned
who isn't here

Who is screaming so terribly
who is silent

Who is without lips

What is this
surfacing
how horrifyingly this small body
grows

all this commotion all these words
who isn't here
it's he
that good boy
has turned
into a thing
which stealthily
comes out of the water
and tears the mother apart

1955

Beyond Words

What are you doing
emerged from darkness
Why don't you want
to live in full light

Within me
war opens up an eyelid
of a million shattered faces

Blood-smeared
what are you piecing together
what is your burden

I am piecing together words
I carry my time

Your sunless toil
has already lasted
so long

One tear
inexpressible
beyond words

Wood

A wooden Christ
from a medieval mystery play
goes on all fours

full of red splinters

he has a collar of thorns
and the bowed head
of a beaten dog

how thirsty and starved this wood is

Golden Mountains

the first time
I saw mountains
I was
twenty-six

In their presence
I didn't laugh
I didn't shout
I spoke in whispers

When I returned home
I meant to tell
mother
what mountains were like

That was difficult to do
at night
everything looks different
including mountains and words

Mother was silent
perhaps tired
she fell asleep

The moon
the golden mountain
of humble folk
waxed in the clouds

1955

Leave Us

Forget us
forget our generation
live like humans
forget us

we envied
plants and stones
we envied dogs

I'd rather be a rat
I told her then

I'd rather not be
I'd rather sleep
and wake when war is over
she said her eyes shut

Forget us
don't enquire about our youth
leave us

1955–57

In the Midst of Life

After the end of the world
after death
I found myself in the midst of life
creating myself
building life
people animals landscapes

this is a table I said
this is a table
there is bread and a knife on the table
knife serves to cut bread
people are nourished by bread

man must be loved
I learnt by night by day
what must one love
I would reply man

this is a window I said
this is a window
there is a garden beyond the window
I see an apple-tree in the garden
the apple-tree blossoms
the blossom falls
fruit is formed
ripens

my father picks the apple
the man who picks the apple
is my father

I sat on the threshold
that old woman who
leads a goat on a string
is needed more
is worth more

than the seven wonders of the world
anyone who thinks or feels
she is not needed
is a mass murderer

this is a man
this is a tree this is bread

people eat to live
I kept saying to myself
human life is important
human life has great importance
the value of life
is greater than the value of all things
which man has created
man is a great treasure
I repeated stubbornly

this is water I said
I stroked the waves with my hand
and talked to the river
water I would say
nice water
this is me

man talked to water
talked to the moon
to the flowers and to rain
talked to the earth
to the birds
to the sky

the sky was silent
the earth was silent
and if a voice was heard
flowing
from earth water and sky
it was a voice of another man

1955

Posthumous Rehabilitation

The dead have remembered
our indifference
The dead have remembered
our silence
The dead have remembered
our words

The dead see our snouts
laughing from ear to ear
The dead see
our bodies rubbing against each other
The dead see our hands
poised for applause

The dead read our books
listen to our speeches
delivered so long ago

the dead hear
clucking tongues

The dead scrutinize our lectures
join in previously terminated
discussions

The dead see stadiums
ensembles and choirs declaiming rhythmically

all the living are guilty

little children
who offered bouquets of flowers
are guilty
lovers are guilty
guilty are poets

guilty are those who ran away
and those that stayed
those who were saying yes
those who said no
and those who said nothing

the dead are taking stock of the living
the dead will not rehabilitate us

1957

Forms

These forms once so well-behaved
obedient always ready to receive
the dead matter of poetry
frightened by fire and the smell of blood
have broken out and dispersed

they attack their creator
tear him apart and drag him
through endless streets
down which have long since gone
all the bands schools and processions

the breathing meat
filled with blood
is still the food
for these perfect forms

they press so close around their spoil
that even silence does not penetrate
outside

December 1956

The King

Alone
when they place before him
a bowl of food
he purrs quivers
licks his chops

a loose bag of bones

you are the lord of creation
—I tell him—
the lion focuses his gaze
when you stare
you are the lord of the world

you are Socrates Caesar
Columbus Shakespeare
you've composed sonnets split the atom
built crematoria
raised Notre Dame

you have opened the snouts
of stone gargoyles
never mind that now
they laugh
at me at you

he runs away
a bone in his jaws
I run after him call

you are the lord of creation
king
and cathedral

1957

Job 1957

Earth sky Job's body dung
sky dung
eyes dung
lips

that which was begot in love
which grew ripened
which was gladsome
is turned to dung

earth sky Job's body
rose dung
lips dung
sky

that which was veiled in caresses
which was robed in dignity
which rose
fell

flies cover
sky and sun
swarm over silence and lips

July 1957

The Door

Builders
had left a vertical opening in the wall
I sometimes think
my home is too conventional
all sorts of people
can easily get in

Had the builders not left
that opening in the wall
I would have become a hermit

alas

I waste my time
coming in and going out
a revolving door has lately been installed
through it
enter the affairs of this world

but neither a blossoming apple-tree
nor a little
moist-eyed pony
neither a star nor a golden hive
neither a stream
teeming with fish nor buttercups
have ever appeared in it

and yet I shan't wall up this door
maybe a good man
will appear in it
and tell me who I am

A Meeting

I meet the dead more and more often
they are strangely animated
their mouths are open they talk a lot
some of them foam
like soap

recently I came across a largish group of the dead
who sat in rows on chairs
their cheeks rosy
they laughed clapped sat down
were indignant got up
made personal remarks

among old corpses
bustled the young
they don't know
they're scatter-brained
they move their arms and legs
drive cars embrace new
standpoints and wives who are still warm

there was one experienced deceased
who kept winking at me
roguishly
and even tried
to be reborn
in the eyes of the assembly

November 1956
(*at the Writers' Congress in Warsaw*)

Conversation with the Prince

1

Fangs have pierced the earth
don't let
the dogs
off the silken thread

howling and squealing
they will tear each other apart
can't you hear
their throats
gurgling

stretched
to the utmost
limits
our well-behaved intentions
tremble

2

That's a faire thought
to ly between Maids
legs

The Prince
expressed
his thoughts and feelings
simply
those learnèd in the scriptures
have obscured everything

That's a fine thought

the world suddenly open

72

your poor relation
Prince oh Prince
one of your attendant Lords
Mr Prufrock noticed
that his bald spot
is growing and fell into
an Hamletic mood

shuffling among
tamed people furniture
calculates the pros & cons
lying between the legs
of a certain lady
he is not free
from reflection
calculates the profit and loss
sweats in terror
thus adding madness
to fear
mixes the taste of desire
with thoughts of rising prices
shuts his eyes sweats and counts

out of his pocket he draws
not a sword but a hand
bites his nails
hides
hides in a scabbard
and screams
to be to be
at any price

3

Do not speak of me
contemptuously Prince
I have good intentions
twice in my dreams

73

I flew in the sky
I know I am a clerk's backside
my mane
my stale anger
is not as you imagine it
from dawn to dusk
I change
continually
I am deferential
you can impress
any mark upon me
you are the seal
I am the wax of the world
Prince my brother Prince
Ophelia
has drawn in
her angel's wings
she is at this moment
giving birth to sinners

4

Prince
I am not a clerk
I am a contemporary
poet
the year is 1958
you are curious to know
what a contemporary poet does

Indifferent
he talks to the indifferent
blinded he signals
to the sightless
he laughs and
barks in his sleep
woken up
he weeps

he is all rungs
but not a Jacob's ladder
he's a voice without an echo
a weightless burden
a kingless fool

You ask about the shape of yonder cloud
'tis like a camel indeed
thou think'st it is like
a weasel
it is back'd like
a weasel
or like a whale?
very like a whale

you laugh at me
good Prince
you detect the windbag
behind the arras

Das Hirn verwest so wie der Arsch*

1960

---

* The brain rots like the arse (Gottfried Benn)

The Return

I can never come to terms
with some of my poems
years pass
I can't come to terms with them
yet I cannot disown them
they are bad but they're mine
I gave them birth
they live away from me
indifferent and dead
but there will come a moment when they all
will rush back to me
the successful and the failures
the crippled and the perfect
the ridiculed and the rejected

they will roll into one

One Can

I recollect that in the past
poets composed 'poetry'
one can still write verses
for many many years
one can also do
many other things

Solution

I am
stubborn
and submissive in my stubbornness
like wax
only thus can I
impress the world

1960

The New Man

The new man
that's him there
yes it's that
sewage pipe
which lets through
everything

White Spots

On the 20th of August
an eighty-year-old woman
suffering from amnesia
and wearing a blue dress
with white spots
disappeared from her home

anyone able to provide any information
about the missing person
is requested

Fear

Your fear is powerful
metaphysical
mine a junior clerk
with a briefcase

with a file
and a questionnaire
when was I born
what means of support
what haven't I done
what don't I believe in

what am I doing here
when will I stop pretending
where will I go
next

Monuments

Our monuments
are ambiguous
they are shaped like a pit

our monuments
are shaped
like a tear

moles
built our monuments
under the earth

our monuments
are shaped like smoke
they go straight to heaven

1960

Completion

This side
is turned towards others
and though it is worn
changeable counterfeit
it gives an idea
of my shape

the other side
which no one knows
which will never see
the light of day
which unto death and after death
will not be touched by others

that other side
known only to me
remains hidden
but influences the side which is
revealed
and through it communicates with other people

who
surprised
amused
appalled

exclaim

fancy his being like that
it's not at all like him
this must be someone else

in the familiar portrait
a new ambiguous feature has appeared
startling
and completing

Shallowly Quicker

I feel desire
he said
unfortunately he has no soul
the soul has gone
burst out laughing
the young waitress
her shape was such
one could soulless
with her create
a new man

honest her arse
is more finely moulded
than
the dome of that famous
cathedral—he thought—
a splendid vessel
temporarily closed

the souls must have been snatched up
by previous generations
and now one has to live
as best one can
shallowly
quicker

Death

Wall window
outside
a child's tiny voice

below the window a street
a tram
King Herod enters
devil death

I give the King sixpence
and chase away
the whole crowd

death
is real
looks back
shakes her finger

It's So Hidden

It's so hidden
it hardly tints
objects
people
landscapes

at a certain moment
(when, I don't know)
it begins to run
together
into one
into one thing
one place
one face

we have to distinguish

that first one
primitive
makes use of
execution squads
insignia and uniforms
it attacks armies nations herds

but that other
so gentle
hidden reminds you perhaps
of love
perhaps of children's games

it enters into the voice
which mentions your name and surname
indistinctly behind a door
or possibly even quite a different
name and surname

it loves nesting
in closed
compartments
envelopes files
railway tickets
summonses and proclamations

it is patient and persistent

it tightens its grip
when you can't breathe
it lets you slip
out of its hands
yes it has hands
you may breathe
you may chat
with a child
and when the child
takes you by the hand
and you think you can go
it stops you
that day it made use of a summons
the letter lay forgotten
for some days
under a pile of papers

in broad daylight
in a house full
of good and well-disposed people
before lunch
it threw itself at me

blows followed
it struck at
the stomach
the throat
the head and the head again
all I had to do was to call

or to open the door
but I was losing breath and speech

when it let go
I was falling

Unrecorded Epistle

But Jesus stooped
and wrote on the sand
then again he stooped
and wrote with his finger

Mother they are so dim
and simple I have to perform
marvels I do such silly
and futile things
but you understand
and forgive your son
I change water into wine
raise the dead
walk the seas

they are like children
one has always
to show them something new
just imagine

And when they approached
he covered and effaced
the letters
for ever

New Comparisons

To what will you compare
day
is it like night
to what will you compare
an apple
is it like a kingdom
to what will you compare
flesh
at night
the silence
between lips
between
to what will you compare an eye
a hand in darkness
is the right like the left
teeth tongue mouth
a kiss
to what will you compare
a hip
hair
fingers
breath
silence
poetry
in daylight
at night

A Fight with an Angel

The shadow of the wings grew
the angel crowed and hummed
his moist
nostrils touched
my eyes lips
we fought on a ground
of trodden newspapers
in a rubbish dump where
saliva blood and bile
lay mixed
with the dung of words

the shadow of the wings grew
there were two
wings
from ear to ear immense
pink
on either side of the head
amid clouds
our excrement covered
the pitch
eventually he overpowered me
tied me up dazzled me and slobbered over me
with words and chatting
optimistically
was ascending into the heaven of poetry
I caught him by the leg
he fell on my dump
under the wall
here I am
a manshaped being
with eyes smashed
to let in
light

1959

Green Rose

'. . . she'd embroidered the rose in green . . .'

Huge cities
grow
overpopulated
become depopulated
the tide rising
and falling
shoals of men
the cities close
to each other
you can see the decay
out of fragments of words
scattered
here and there
you can imagine the interior
but in the swarm
without the queen
our loneliness increases
the distance from man to
grows beneath the neons
in overpopulated cities
rubbing against each other drawing blood
we live on an island
peopled by a handful of creatures
we are left with a few closest to us
but they too depart
each in his own way
they take with them
vacuum cleaners insipid paintings
women children
motors fridges
a stock of information
ashes pseudonyms
remnants of an aesthetic
a faith

something resembling God
something resembling love
still others
depart to their caves
with meat in their teeth
the weaker remain
in bars at tables
the weaker still
lean on shadows of words
but these words are so transparent
you can see death through them
never mind
we are leaving
dragging our feet tight-lipped
and nobody admits he is leaving
better not create havoc
so all live for ever

you remember
we were open
in the times of the greatest oppression
another's suffering and another's joy
easily penetrated our interiors
your lives sped towards me
on all sides
now we are covered in armour
only through cracks
in our faces
can we see

In the Light of Day

Others are still
sitting comfortably
in the darkness
a sweet in every inside
they wait
for the comedy or drama

On the white sheet
women with eyes
that open and close
with lips
teeming with white teeth
undress
before the eyes of the assembled

blood flows
out of open bodies
along with the music
and the dialogue

here everything is
amusing shocking
more interesting
more beautiful
than in the real world
suddenly diminished
deprived of flavour

When the hero strangles
the heroine
or covers her
with kisses
the consumers stop sucking
their sweets
they sit with parted lips
their faces turned

to the white cloth
which secretes
a phosphorescent sheen

In the light of day
a real tear
looks small and colourless
that real woman
walking by the wall
looks ugly
weeping
her nose red
her eyelashes without colour
gummed together
the stocking on her left leg
is crumpled

To the Heart

I watched
an expert cook
he would thrust his hand
into the windpipe
pushing it through
into the sheep's
inside
and there in the quick
would grasp the heart
his fingers closing
round the heart
would rip out the heart
with one pull
yes
he certainly was an expert

1959

Proposition the Second

The poem
is finished
now to break it
and when it grows together again
break it once more
at places where it meets reality
remove the joints
the random elements
which come from the imagination
those that remain
tie up
with silence
or leave untied
when
the poem is finished
remove the foundation
on which it rests
—for foundations
restrict movement—
then the construction
will rise
and for a moment
will soar above reality
with which eventually
it will collide
the collision
will be the birth
of a new poem
a stranger to reality
surprising
splitting
and transforming it

and itself undergoing
a transformation

Mars

A room

a family
of five or six

someone's reading a book
someone's looking at photographs
someone remembers the war
someone's falling asleep someone leaves
someone's dying in the silence
someone's drinking water
someone's breaking bread
Tommy writes the letter A
and draws a knight with a blue spur
someone's getting ready to go to the moon
someone's brought a rose a bird a fish
it's snowing
a bell tolls

Mars appears
his sword
fills the room
with fire

They Shed the Load

He comes to you
and says

you are not responsible
either for the world or the end of the world
the load has been lifted off your shoulders
you are like children and birds
go, play

and they play

they forget
that contemporary poetry
means struggle for breath

1959

A Late 19th Century Love Poem

Two legs or four legs
Legs over the head
Legs on the back
Legs on the shoulders
Legs thrown in the air
Legs running away

A leg bent
At the knee
Cancancancancancancancancancan

A red shoe behind glass
a golden slipper
a patent-leather shoe
an upturned moustache
more ferarum*

a knee a lioness
the stocking unbuttoned
between the fingers
had I been younger my dear
a gartered thigh
upturned moustaches
a beard a strap a matron
legs crossed
hem of a dress a maiden
black moustaches trembling
leg in bath
leg on a tree
leg on a ladder
a darling leg
I kiss your hand
between the piano's legs
stand corsets lampshades
artificial flowers stars
stuffed eagles falcons
phoney Gothic cathedrals

December 1959

* in the manner of wild beasts

I Was Writing

I wrote
for a moment or an hour
dusk night
I grew angry
trembled or sat
dumb by my own side
eyes filled with tears
I'd been writing a good while
suddenly I noticed
no pen in my hand

Et in Arcadia Ego

*Und wie man sagt, dass einer, dem ein Gespenst erschienen,
nicht wieder froh wird, so konnte man umgekehrt von ihm
sagen, dass er nie ganz unglücklich werden konnte, weil er
sich immer widder nach Neapel dachte.*—GOETHE*

TRANSMIGRATION OF SOULS

It was noon
in a nameless street

the sun struck him

he walked along a deserted street
a gust of wind
swept papers and rubbish
which rustled and grated
human skin cigarette stubs
the skins of Mediterranean fruit
rot velvet
mouths open
posters have beautiful white teeth

now there are people everywhere

a huge building beside it
another huge building
a red table shaded by an awning
at a white table a huge belly a cut-off head
resting between arms
sleeps and floats

* And just as it is said of someone who has seen a ghost
that he will never again be happy, so contrariwise one
can say of someone that he will never be unhappy so
long as he thinks of Naples.

a red-hot tile under the foot

boys ran up to him
angels in coloured stripes
circles triangles palms
a cherub with ruby lips
and dirty ears

they came to him
grabbed his suitcase
others snatched it from them
into his hand they slipped cards
handbills street-plans

cards bearing the names of hotels

they walked beside him behind him
in front of him
repeated names
cried and spoke with their hands
lifted their hands
folded and unfolded their hands
a man in a white shirt
made a sign of the cross

they left him half-closed their eyes
flashed the whites of their eyes sang
behind him strayed two admirals
and a queen's page

that was splendid theatre
behind him lay
Stazione Centrale Napoli

silence
he stopped in the shade of a tree
no there was no tree
he stopped
in the shade of a lorry

99

the shade drove away

the sun struck him

the street was emptying
he wiped his face with his hand
he wiped his hands with a handkerchief
the handkerchief smelled
of orange peel
he walked ahead
reached a square
a statue stood in the square

another lay on a bench
a newspaper over his face
another statue
in bright socks
his shoes under the bench
on the pedestal
the head of an unknown hero
dripped with hoary bird-droppings
he had a sabre and a spur
that third one under the statue
who was feeding the pigeons
had no sabre
he wore a shoe with a heavy
heel
a hoof

streets converged
and diverged in the twinkling of an eye
he stood paralysed asking for a name
was shown many streets
was shown the way
people smiled hurried on
hurried on were polite
two girls
with two tongues licked
heaps of ice-cream with warm

tongues they licked white and pink
ices

bunches of lemons hung
with rigid lacquered leaves
bananas lay curved
patched with black
brown figs
pink melons moons
of water and light in a hippo skin
with rows of pips in the mouth
next to that head lay a second head
head on top of head and head next to head
a pyramid of heads rose
up to the whitened sky
blind heads of coconuts
covered with tawny hair
crushed with saliva in a white interior
the dented rim of a stone vessel
of an extinct volcano
a dark mountain over a transparent bay
stirred and came to him
came to his feet
threw an arc
he was motionless

this was the house
in it a third-rate
pensione
a lift took him up
a grille of iron branches
a white-haired woman
leads him along a corridor
opens a door smiles
points to two beds
joined together
gives him a key
smiles leaves

the shutters are closed
stripes of light tremble
like a zebra at a water hole
two beds in the mirror he looks
at his face in the mirror half-closes
his eyes a lamp near the ceiling
lamps and faces in mirrors
coloured towels on chrome rails
a mirror over the basin
newspapers in the drawer
left by the guest who went today
an hour ago a hairpin
it was a woman

a stream
of water lukewarm water
cooling water flows noisily
down his open
hands he turns the key

hangers swing in the wardrobe
in the wardrobe smelling of a stranger
hangers hum
wooden metal arms
stripped of dresses
he lay down closed his eyes
he lies under a white sheet
thoughts crumble
the thread which ties
images and words snaps
you don't know what to do with me
only let me unpack
close your eyes I want to change
you can't close your eyes
you think you're being funny
I brought a letter from Frank
what is scampi you are a scamp
you said you would take me with you
but you left so suddenly

here I am in this godforsaken dump
who knows if I'm still alive

look who is here what are you doing here
have you been here long how long are you here for
what's the news from Warsaw
ah you've got a grant
I had a feeling
you were hiding from us
among those marble statues
wonderful paintings

we are in Venice together
I can't believe it
kiss me
you are Polish
let's have a drink
I'm alone in the world

he wakes terrified

this room but what house
this house but what city
this reflection but what mirror
that city
is it still there
beyond the wall
it talks to itself
where is Naples
this is Naples
such is Naples
there is your Naples
see Naples and die
how hot it is here
how his feet burn
the flesh scalded
by that white linen
see Naples
through the windows one can see roofs

and walls and windows in walls
and flat roofs in the sky
the white clouded tin of the sky
turning blue
the clanking and roar of motors
what are they doing there
burrowing a hole through the earth
through this house
and if that city is not there beyond the wall
if it is not there
there is only heat in a void
noise rotting fish
machine drills cracking
the surface the concrete breaking
cries songs words too many words
baroque churches of words
dust rustling of papers
and if he is not there
only a cloud a whirl
of noise burning white
an exploding and fading ball
a magician's glass ball
and inside that idiot with a colossal head
beneath the locked cathedral
his head dripping saliva
a bellowing bell hung from a spider's web
that city is falling

terrified he woke
there was night in the mirror

he closed the door behind him

a black sky towered above the street
stars in the sky
tangled neons
the statue was dark
all vehicles
drove towards him

drove around
around the unknown hero
pneumatic hammers and drills
were shattering the concrete crust
the flat square disgorged
shining dust
ashes lava
neon lights flowed
down vertical walls of the sky
women lay in pools of light
black and shining seals
fat multi-eyed red
shining red and silver
with huge bellies they swam
softly in silk
a dwarf leads a soldier by the hand
her face like an apple of paradise
she snaps at her mates
who black silky
stand bloated with light
captive balloons
stars fall
stars with parted lips

youths surround the juke-box
the juke-box sobs and shakes
the juke-box laughs and sings
the juke-box filled
with music and voices
souls migrate
leave the young bodies
enter the juke-boxes
those innocent souls
that don't know sin
don't know penance
automatons are innocent
automatons don't know sin
automatons will not be damned
automatons can't rot

souls migrate in the rain
leave the young bodies
enter the bodies of stars
upon huge posters
all those sceneries of paradise
are sceneries of hell

the church is still open
altars are lit
on the altar behind glass lies a blessed
skeleton in liturgical garb
bones in slippers and gloves
bones in violet stockings
the face gilded
alms-boxes by the prie-dieus
alms-boxes in front of altars
alms-boxes at entrance and exit
for St Anthony's bread
for the beatification of a servant of the Lord
for candles for the Babe
a lamp for the Heart of Jesus
a huge ancient padlock
upon a liver-coloured wall the legend
SS Messe per le Anime del Purgatorio

bodies are saved
bodies belong to the animal world
bodies are innocent
the spirit has found refuge
in the Banco di Santo Spirito
and abandoned bodies
wander through the great city
beneath the opaque sky
beneath the black sky
beneath the lemon sun
bodies are always innocent
while souls gradually shrink
now so tiny that a couple
find room on the tip of the tongue

of that quayside whore
let no one cast a stone upon her
it's Eve driven out of Eden
driven out of a sixteenth-century tapestry
La creazione di Eva
and the eyes of them both were opened
and they knew they were naked
and he placed at the east of the garden of Eden
Cherubim and a flaming sword which turned every way
to keep the way of the tree of life

'We find ourselves at the end of an era
the musician perishes as did the poet'
the poet who perished thinks
woman is like a flower
lay aside
that beautiful
ancient simile
a flower that smiles
a flower that fears
a flower with a flower in her hair
a flower which sells itself
a flower which comes and goes
a woman is like a woman
a flower is like a flower
word has become flesh
flesh fills the night
from shore to shore
night has no shores
a woman is like a flower
lay aside
that beautiful
ancient simile

under electric lights
nutty heads of coco-
nuts
hairy heads of blind apes
small peeled bananas

lemony lemons with black leaves
a spark of light sprinkles the glass
the chrome the colours of drinks
blocks of ice open oysters on ice
the spark of light on a slice of lemon
light drowns in the ice
drowns continually
people hand money stretch out their palms
put in nets and newspapers
tiny fish like open penknives
navy-blue tuna patterned with tree-rings
the head of a sleeping jellyfish the legs of an octopus
guts lie on the ice
on green leaves
like dead lambs
vermilion liver
hearts and tongues
and curious fish
with heads like red hammers
like blue hedgehogs
flat like discs
with golden skins
black roe sparkles
under electric light
birds so many birds
so many birds on a wire
piercing their silent throats
threading their open beaks

Midnight time to go back
a jet lances the sky over the bay
beneath angelic hairs of light
Englishwomen pass
with their white necks they laugh
doves sleep sweetly
at the hero's feet
lemons of light roll over the sea
a sailor stands with hands in his pockets
the body of a quayside 'seagull'

so pathetic between the sheets
tiny like the body of a child
a yellow parchment with black eyes
a woman with her young
sleeps on the temple steps
she has covered them up with a newspaper
in a blind alley the heart of Jesus
pierced with a sword in a garland of fairy-lights
a musician replaces his violin
in its case
sits at a table
waiters fold the cloths
sails
over the bay stars and palms
tomorrow the sun will explode
over the city

tomorrow a military parade

2 BLOCCO PER NOTE

Night at the Albergo Fiore
NAPOLI
I look through my notes

Time present
is an excellent murderer
of the past
the cruellest because not tied to
its victim
Vienna airport
a chap smiles at the sausages
das ist schön he says
to the sausages
a Japanese pours pills
into his palm like grains of rice
a bearded Hindu
lost in meditation

passes by

In the Vatican Museum
Sobieski at Vienna
the guide informs American matrons
about the Polish king who has just
defeated the Turks at the gates of Vienna
and freed the Austrian capital
Entrance to the cupola
Eingang zur Kuppel
Ingresso alla Cupola
the guides hurriedly copulate
with the beauty in the tourists' eyes
this union brings forth
bored monsters
smiling giraffes
they remove shoes
from aching feet

Yesterday I met
an acquaintance from Warsaw
this was as beautiful as
'a chance encounter upon a dissecting
table of a sewing machine with
an umbrella'

that pietà that pietà that pietà
Pietà di Michelangelo
is this pietà this pietà this pietà
an original in original marble
but of course

Kolossal fantastisch er fliegt
refers to God the Father
in the Sistine Chapel

Somebody came
somebody interrupted
I lost the thread

in Rome
in the Sistine Chapel
such a crowd noisier
than a railway station
Michelangelo's Last Judgement
is being admired
is it beauty
I don't know how to express
this shock
I had to rest my head on the back of a seat

in the Sistine Chapel
I saw a blind man
his wife Eve
his eye
led him by the hand
she whispered descriptions
The Last Judgement
The Creation of the World
The Creation of Adam
The Exile from Paradise
He lifted up his face
voices fell
on his eyes removed into
darkness
while I multi-eyed multi-eared
open on all sides
gobbled voices and colours
women
on perches
lay eggs of beauty
my head has split
with the buzz

on May 21st at noon
I visited the Baths of Caracalla
I am sorry about this chaos
but the world emerged from chaos
let all this create itself

in movement
did you think
I would return quite changed
no need to pretend

what is the share of beauty
per head
upon earth
what share of truth per head
meat digests meat
the crisis of contemporary civilization
has lasted so long
but I suspect there is no crisis
I am carnivorous
would you like a leg or a breast
shall I serve steak tartare
we are the bulwark
I order a tartare the Tartar invasions*
death of the flower of knighthood
garnish the steak
you've ordered yes I've ordered a tartare
Et in Arcadia ego
you too pretend to be Don Quixote
those wingless windmills
are ordinary chalets
please come closer
you twist my words
what share of meat what share of truth
per head
which falls
they questioned me in the night
your last wish
somebody replied for me
a glass of champagne
turned towards the wall and died

* Poland was Christendom's bulwark in the defence
against Tartar invasions which ravaged the country
regularly over four centuries from 1240. (TRANS.)

'Compared with historical events
of a political or military character
everything else seems trivial'
says F. M.
'All you can do in a waiting room
is read newspapers'

Write a treatise
about identity
in new poetry

reality
is filled
with reality
through cracks in reality
imagination may filter
'an imagined illusion arises within us
through which we sometimes grasp
the similarities of things as things in themselves
this happens with sleepers and madmen'

Must not leave a single space
a single blank space
for imagination

at a press conference
the painter S. D.
emerges from a gigantic egg
or appears in a dinner jacket
covered with eighty-eight
glasses each filled with
Crème de Menthe
one contains a dead fly
this wouldn't impress me
I've seen various things
but let's return to my Italian journey
on May 21st at noon
I visited the Baths of Caracalla
the sun

melted me down and sucked me up
the sun on my head
above me in the sky
lie brick mammoths
poppies bloom by the walls
the walls are singing
swallows' nests
a ginger cat like a bone
gazes with a turquoise eye
red poppies in the grass
under the bare foot cool
smooth pebbles in the shade
rows of chairs
columns pillars capitols
of plaster and hardboard
performances are held here at night
a huge plane flew past
the cat ran his way
those women walked by again
I had seen them in the catacombs
Catacombe di S. Callisto
the catacombs were quite jolly
the trattoria S. Callisto
is directly opposite
prices are high the position is good
that woman in a black dress
is like a snake
in American or English skin
a zip down the back
the snake is done up with a hook
wish I could see it change its skin
waiters like cabbage whites
flutter around the table
stretch out their wings
with black dots
after lunch you can go down
into the catacombs
but why
it's fun being here

never mind the martyrs
there is no sun under the earth
am I to pluck out my eye
which has been offending me for the past hour
it's all the fault
of that gorgeous reptile
I draw a fish on the table
but she must be
a pagan not the fish of course
she passes by
a bouquet of the five senses
at that moment I have a hundred senses
all stimuli are prodding me
they are real bulls
waiters with red cloths
run around
stuff me with figures
I am stained with wine
above me in the sun
their tongues protrude
dripping saliva

On June 22nd 1960
I got out at the railway station
in Venice
'In Venedig kennt mich vielleicht
nur ein Mensch, und der wird
mir nicht gleich begegnen'*
here a star
was my home
a star above a black canal
at night I opened the window
a golden third-rate star
it rained
this is the name of my hotel

* In Venice there is perhaps only one man who knows
me, and we are unlikely to meet.

Notturno sul Canal Grande

in a paper bag I glide
down a less representative canal
instead of lights and streamers
rubbish flew out of a window
it flies falls floats
nobody sings here
there are few lights the scents less refined
yesterday I wept
it was so beautiful
or perhaps I laughed
my ghosts were asleep
at Torcello I saw a beautiful hell
on the basilica's walls
I bought two sea-horses
they smell of salt and seaweed
they bring happiness
so I am happy

St Mark's Basilica
a girl covers up her shoulders
and head with black lace
that other one in jeans
stands damned by the guard
at the temple's door
an unclean vessel
Satan's handiwork
in those red pantaloons
clinging tight for temptation

Venice burns
rain Tintoretto gold
rain falls greenery
Tintoretto midnight
pigeons and white orchestras sleep
the Lido burns and I hear
the crack of neon branches
in the cooled sand

moulds of bodies
now departed

huge effigies with monstrous heads
laugh noiselessly from ear to ear
and a maid too beautiful for me
an inhabitant of a small town in the North
rides astride an ichthyosaurus
Objects excavated in my country have small black
heads sealed with plaster and horrible grins

3 MILITARY PARADE

Albergo Fiore
the owner woke me up
good morning
my name's Kowalczyk
after the war I stayed here in Naples
the general says to me
(that was in Łódź before the war)
sergeant have a drink with me
I am on duty sir
I invite you says the general

we have a military parade today
are you going to see it
yes today I will watch the parade
tomorrow Pompeii and Vesuvius
thank you Mr Kowalczyk

Trucks drive past
soldiers sit in the trucks
they sit one next to the other
in steel helmets they sit in rows
weapons glisten in the sun
trucks follow one another
all identical
identical soldiers

sit in identical trucks
their faces hidden
truck after truck
the roar of engines white tyres

someone unknown has wound it all up
everything moves efficiently

the tank's turret is open
the pennant flutters in the wind
the tanks are heavy and huge
the barrels of guns dark silent
radio masts glisten
tank after tank rattles by
armoured cars
spiked with machine-guns
and batteries of guns
a helicopter shines in the sky
the armoured cars and tanks
make a gentle curve
then come red lorries
red lorry after red lorry
all well wound-up
then guns pontoons and tractors
children and girls rejoice
and even serious people
who have been in hell

and then handsome soldiers
handsome soldiers run lightly
feathers stream in the wind
black white red
feathers run soldiers fly
someone has wound up the vehicles and the people
the parade unfolds
in the sun over the blue bay
a beautiful colourful army runs
black feathers fly
bands play soldiers dance

surely no one here will kill
that soldier in the tank
is beautiful as an angel
he will never burn

from the hill the city ascends to the sky
in the sky Pompeian red
glistens like open lungs
above the transparent bay

'Der Neapolitaner
glaubt im Besitz des Paradieses zu sein
und hat von den nördlichen Ländern
einen sehr traurigen Begriff;
Sempre neve, case di legno,
gran ignoranza . . .
Immer Schnee, holzerne Häuser,
grosse Unwissenheit . . .'*

    ★

Tell me about
your Italian journey

I am not ashamed
I wept in that country

beauty touched me

I was a child once more
in the womb of that country
I wept
I am not ashamed

I have tried to return to paradise

1960–61

---

* The Neapolitan believes that he lives in Paradise, and is very sorry for
the lands of the North; always snow, wooden houses, great ignorance.

'In a cathedral . . .'

In a cathedral
in the rose
in lead
your white nape
hewn from darkness

when you were lifting up your face
your lips caught by your teeth
bled

on that side
parted lips
shone

a whisper floats up
damp and warm from your interior
it penetrates the conch of your ear

the tongue moves

lips part
a blow with the chopper

from the night
along the body
to the white spine
of dawn

a blind
desire wakens in the blind
stirs
spawns
a hand in a hand
spawns a tongue in the mouth
hair
a hand in the hair fingers

Nothing in Prospero's Cloak

Caliban slave
instructed in human speech
waits

snout in dung
feet in paradise
he sniffs man
waits

nothing comes
nothing in Prospero's
magic robes
nothing from
streets and lips
from pulpits and towers
nothing from loudspeakers
speaks to nothing
about nothing

nothing begets nothing
nothing brings up nothing
nothing awaits nothing
nothing threatens
nothing condemns
nothing pardons

1962

At the Same Time

At this time
the long galleries of the Louvre
are empty

At the same time
Les Halles
bleed in the electric light
the mound of meat
the monstrous cadaver
twitched
in the open belly
in the din
a thorn of light pokes
and intestines steam
through an opening in the face

At this same time
there are no eyes
among the paintings
no one experiences
no one consumes beauty
only the Gioconda
smiles
mysteriously and laboriously

1958–61

The Smile of Leonardo da Vinci

God fell

lies on his back
defenceless
his life
eternal
stands revealed

dragged
by intelligent ants
to his grave a live
beetle
black shining
his shield-like head
in a golden halo

Man lifts him with a straw

and watches
with a mysterious
smile
on his lips

as that other
coleopterous
and dark

flies away

1962

A Lesson in Patience

For Mieczysław Porębski

The Wall of China
I touched it with the fingers of both hands
the centre of this landscape is a song of a bird
the centre of this city is a woman's smile
the landscape falls apart
the city falls away like meat from the bone
leaving a smile
the Wall of China
I scrambled on its back
like the back of a sleeping god
I saw it with my own eyes
without beginning or end

there was a time when women gave birth to slaves
imprisoned from head to foot
they bore mousetraps
the sea is
vast and immense blue fetters which have fallen

I reminisce about the Wall
it's been raining all day
it's been raining so long
that I think of the Wall of China
of the spine of an extinct dynasty
of the smile of Buddha
with the eyes of tiny Chu-Lin
who had green ribbons in her plaits

I saw it from below
it resembled the life of a poet
and the life of a clerk
it resembled nothing
I saw it once more from a bird's-eye view

from the window
of a plane

that Wall divided
nothing defended nothing stretched on
there was a time when women gave birth to small
and large prisons
cages in which a heart was beating
the sea immense jangling fetters
throws up corpses
with pink feet

that Wall provides an object lesson
for people unable to imagine
the nature of the imagination
of reality

When they asked me
what the Wall is like
I replied with a smile
it's long I have not seen its beginning
or end
and then I added it's very long

From a Biography

date of birth
place of birth
Radomsko 1921

yes
this leaf
from my son's schoolbook
contains my biography
there's still a little space left
there are some blanks

I crossed out just two sentences
but added one
in a little while
I shall write in a few words

you ask about
the more significant events and dates
in my life
ask others

my biography almost came to an end
on several occasions
some better some worse

1965

Laughter

The cage stayed shut
until a bird was hatched inside

the bird remained mute
until the cage
rusting in the silence
opened

silence lasted until
behind black wires
we heard laughter

The First is Hidden

the first tree

I don't remember
its name
nor the landscape
where it grew

I don't remember
whether I came to know it
with my eye
or ear
whether it was a rustle
a scent or a hue

whether it appeared
in sunlight
or in snow

the first animal

I don't remember
its voice warmth
shape

all animals
have their names

only that first one
is hidden
unknown

1965

Doors

A glass of red wine
stands on a table
in a dark room

through the open door
I see a landscape of childhood
a kitchen and a blue kettle
the Sacred Heart
mother's transparent shadow

the crowing cock
in a rounded silence

the first sin
a little white seed
in a green fruit soft
bitterish

the first devil is pink
and moves its hemispheres
under a spotted silk

dress
in the illumined landscape
a third door
opens
and beyond it in a mist
towards the back
a little to the left
or in the centre

I see
nothing

1966

I Build

I tread on a pane
on a mirror
that cracks

I tread on Yorick's
skull
I tread on this brittle
world

and build a house
a castle in the air
within all's ready
for a siege

only I
remain surprised
outside
the walls

'The sea at night . . .'

The sea at night
broke
booming
crashed
its frame
against puny concrete
breakwaters
at sunset
purring

it stretched along the beaches
reconciled
it covered itself
with purple
still trembling angrily
glistened
beneath the waves' skin

Gagra, 1965

Leda

Leda with strong
arms
and thighs

Leda pressed
against the bird's
supple body

her head thrown back
a mysterious smile
absent
she receded

I was torn away
from her
pushed aside

blood
flowed
from
my lips and tongue

1965

In a Strange Tongue

She was selling fruit

for me
her words
were sealed

I pointed
to a pomegranate
and asked her
to open it

a ripe interior
bled in sunlight

the mouth
flashed with a moist smile
filled with
teeth tongue
and words
of a strange flavour

1968

Penetration

death
penetrated life
like light
through a cobweb
hanging in an open doorway

now on his death-bed

he was moving out
shouting plotting stratagems
temporizing

death was eating up the features
of successive faces layered
on the bone

Draft for a Contemporary Love Poem

For surely whiteness
is best described through greyness
bird through stone
sunflowers
in December

in the past love poems
described flesh
described this and that
eyelashes for instance

surely redness
should be described
through greyness sun through rain
poppies in November
lips at night

the most telling
description of bread
is one of hunger
it includes
the damp porous centre
the warm interior
sunflowers at night
breasts belly thighs of Cybele

a spring-like
transparent description
of water
is the description of thirst
of ashes
desert
it conjures up a mirage
clouds and trees enter
the mirror

Hunger deprivation
absence
of flesh
is the description of love
the contemporary love poem

Summer 1963

Butterflies

it was raining
rain fell

the reporter was talking about Florence
rising from the waters

about Florence of mud and slime
covered with oil-stains
a pearl
a pearl of cities he was saying
five thousand cars
carried off by the mad waves of the Arno
ten thousand cars
buried in the mud
jewels paintings
clocks
manuscripts maps
were swept out by the waves

135

I was last
in Florence
in June 1964

I drank wine
by the Arno
shallow clouded yellow
like a dog's eye
grizzly clouds
were moving through your eyes
in the long gallery
a golden
body
stretched in sleep
Venus
woken by Titian
floated her hand upon her dark delta
past the tourists' faces

young
radiant
women
appeared
under a granite colonnade
in ballroom gowns
unearthly creations

a hand
with almond
silver
nails
rested against the grey column
they raised their arms
they skipped on stone steps
they twisted their bodies threw back their heads
froze to a standstill
repeated the same gesture
smiled
raised their faces to heaven

they had painted eyes
starry
huge eyes

nobody accosted them
nobody touched them
they did not speak
they did not sweat
they listened attentively
to a screaming
fat man in an unbuttoned shirt

once more
a girl
in a pink dress
pushed the granite column away
her lips parted

I repeated
after an Old Poet:

'. . . your charm stirs to life in my eye
whene'er I behold a pink hyacinth in bloom . . .
you wore this flower in your golden hair,
it glistened in their midst unespied
like the pink shell of a maiden's shame
in the fresh Spring of her youthful years . . .'

another
in a banana-coloured suit
swung a gleaming
red handbag
gazed into the distance
upon green hills
upon the yellow Arno

once more she threw back her face
once more she was entering the light
once more

137

they were repeating everything
from the beginning

they adjust their hair raise their arms
shaved armpits
parted lips
legs
fixed boldly
wide
apart

In woodland glades
upon heather
meadows and thistles in gardens
Peacocks Painted Ladies Meadow Browns
Dingy Skipper
Adonis Blue
Red Admiral Ringlet Orange Tip and Brimstone

Butterflies seen in childhood
stretch their wings in the sun
at night

1967

Busy with Many Jobs

Busy with very urgent jobs
I forgot
one also has
to die

irresponsible
I kept neglecting that duty
or performed it
perfunctorily

as from tomorrow
things will be different

I'll start dying meticulously
wisely optimistically
without wasting time

Capitulation

For H.M.E.

upon all
my towers dreams
words
and silence
white flags flutter

upon my hate
upon my love
and poetry
white flags are fixed

from all
battlements landscapes
the past
and the future
I hung out white flags

upon faces
and names
upon ascents and falls
white flags flutter

from all my windows
white flags flow

in all my hands
I hold white flags

1966

Poem of Pathos

They spat on the poet
for centuries
they will be wiping the earth and stars
for centuries
they will be wiping their own faces

A poet buried alive
is like a subterranean river
he preserves within
faces names
hope
and homeland

A deceived poet
hears voices
hears his own voice
looks around
like a man woken
at dawn

But a poet's lie
is multilingual
as monumental
as the Tower of Babel

it is monstrous
and does not die

1967

Proofs

Death will not correct
a single line of verse
she is no proof-reader
she is no sympathetic
lady editor

a bad metaphor is immortal

a shoddy poet who has died
is a shoddy dead poet

a bore bores after death
a fool keeps up his foolish chatter
from beyond the grave

In the Theatre of Shades

From the crack
between me and the world
between me and the object
from the distance
between noun and pronoun
poetry
struggles to emerge

it has to make
for itself such tools
shape such forms
as would hook on to me
and the word
like two shores
which diverge
continually

torn apart
it tries once again to
bring together
compare
unite
it struggles
to the surface

I go away

1963

'he tears easily . . .'

he tears easily
like newsprint
roughly patchily

all attempts at glueing him together
get nowhere

he tears up
vertically
from larynx
to rectum

they tore away a strip
on the other side
to make him straighter
but suddenly that other side
appeared longer
he was dropping
and coming apart in their hands
there was a little scrap left
round the spine

shreds of tongue remained
but mildew reached
the roof of the mouth

they crammed a 'philosophy'
down his throat
then cleared up and removed
the paper porridge

A Tale of Old Women

I like old women
ugly women
evil women

they are the salt of the earth

human refuse
does not disgust them

they know the other side
of the coin
of love
and faith

coming and going
dictators clown
their hands stained
with human blood

old women rise at dawn
buy meat fruit bread
clean cook
stand in the street
arms folded silent

old women
are immortal

Hamlet rages in the net
Faust's role is comic and base
Raskolnikov strikes with his axe

old women are
indestructible
they smile indulgently

a god dies
old women get up as usual
buy fish bread and wine
civilization dies
old women get up at dawn
open windows
and remove the filth
a man dies
they wash the corpse
bury the dead
plant flowers
on graves

I like old women
ugly women
evil women

they believe in life everlasting
they are the salt of the earth
the bark of trees
and the humble eyes of beasts

cowardice and heroism
greatness and pettiness
they perceive in true perspective
scaled to demands
of common day

their sons discover America
perish at Thermopylae
die on crosses
conquer the cosmos

old women go out at dawn
to buy milk bread meat
they season the soup
and open the windows

only fools laugh
at old women
ugly women
evil women

for these are beautiful women
good women
old women
they are the embryo
mystery devoid of mystery
the sphere which rolls

old women
are the mummies
of sacred cats

they are tiny
shrivelled
parched
spring's fruit
or plump
oval Buddhas

when they die
a tear
flows from the eye
and joins
the smile
on a young girl's lips

1963

Précis

I look at the window
rain in the dark
crowns of trees
below golden
lupins bloom
I tell my son about Hamlet
I describe the ghost which
a rat behind an arras
an amiable gossip
the father of a demented girl

I think of the Queen Mother's
smooth and milky thighs
the mystery
which the maturing son
espied
love grew and rotted
in him
it had to be poisoned
it had to be lopped off
so he struck with his sword blindly
it had to be bitten off
so he bit it
it had to be drowned like a blind
puppy
so he condemned to death
an innocent girl
I dispense hazy information
about Shakespeare's life
on 3rd July 1962
yet another man on earth
learns
of the English dramatist's existence
rain is falling there is laughter

behind the wall a mouse is scuffling
in the forests silvery moss
is swelling like a drowned man
I pass over in silence
the question
which
the Danish Prince had asked himself
it's a joke too cruel and vulgar
for modern man

1963

Curtains in My Plays

Curtains
in my plays
do not rise
and do not fall
they do not veil
they don't unveil

they rust
moulder rattle
rip

the first is iron
the second rag
the third paper

they drop off
bit by bit

on the heads of
actors
and spectators

curtains in my plays
droop
on the stage
in the auditorium
in the dressing-rooms

even after the show is over
they stick to the feet
rustle and
squeak

1967

Solution

Feeble we live
in a closed orbit
of faces
words and names

others describe us
classify us
pin us down

we know we have to break
to cross the false circle
and go

but we remain

In 1880 in Aden
Rimbaud
ordered various books
including
The Perfect Metalworker
The Pocket Carpenter
or something of that sort
manuals
about firing bricks glass-blowing
candle-dipping
mining
metal-welding
bricklaying
sewage

yes he really had
departed
yet he too
saved
in order to get home
after the death of poetry

he planned to start
a real solid family
devote himself
to bringing up a son
(who naturally was to be
the brave new man)
he also planned
to establish his attitude to army service
on a proper footing
and so on
and so on

that's fine

but tell me
what is
a fifty- sixty-
eighty-year-old
Rimbaud to do

what books
is he to order
where is he to go
what is he to burn
and what abandon

I Clenched My Hand

I clenched my hand
I clenched it
and halted
the shadows

they flit
through the hands
they seep
through the fingers

cold flames
they still drink
they still speak

letters keep coming
Franz Kafka
wrote on 16 March 1913
in a love-letter
to Felice Bauer
'sie streiten in der Küche
über eine gestohlene Wurst
und stören mich'*

I ring up the dead

they open they close
open
doors

in abandoned dovecotes
yellow butterflies
and cobwebs
soak up the sun

* In the kitchen they fight over a stolen sausage and
disturb me

I tried to make you come
to sunny Italy
but last week you died
and were buried

24 December 1967

Knowledge

Nothing will ever be
explained
nothing levelled
nothing rewarded

nothing
never

time will not heal anything
wounds will not scar
a word will not take
the place of another word

grass will not cover up the graves
the dead will die
and will not rise again

the world will not come to an end

poetry will drag itself
on
towards Arcady
or the opposite way

Upon the Departure of a Poet
and a Passenger Train

For Jerzy Lisowski

He doesn't know
what his last poem will be like
nor
what the first day will be like
in a world without poetry

it will probably be raining
there will be a performance of Shakespeare
and tomato soup for lunch

or chicken soup with noodles
a performance of Shakespeare
and rain

the muses gave him no assurance
that with his last breath
he will utter an uplifting thought
lucid
more light and so on

in all probability
he will depart
just like
an overdue
passenger train
from Radomsko to Paris
via Zebrzydowice

1967

Birth of a New Poem

Two poems
rush through the night
thrown
at each other

the shapes of these poems
are modern
precise
the interiors lit up
comfortable and experimental

they fall upon each other
blind

images
routed
cracked
taut
pulverized
penetrated
expiring forms
break the line
stifle breaths
wrench away words
dissolve features

a collision
a new poem
a third poem
born in agony
flows through
the foetal waters
of humanity

the newborn
with a puzzling smile
hidden
poised for sudden
growth

1967

My Poetry

explains nothing
clarifies nothing
makes no sacrifices
is not all-embracing
does not redeem any hopes

does not create new rules of the game
takes no part in play
has a defined place
which it has to fulfil

if it's not a cryptic language
if it speaks without originality
if it holds no surprises
evidently this is how things ought to be

obedient to its own necessity
its range and limitations
it loses even against itself

it does not usurp the space of another poetic
nor can it be replaced by any other
open to all
devoid of mystery

it has many tasks
to which it will never do justice

1965

On the Surface and Inside a Poem

A white mound of salt
on a glass saucer
finger traces
dimple shadows
sparks of tiny crystals

White salt
on a saucer
finger dimples
shadows
sparkling (of light)

salt
on a saucer
finger traces
lights shadows
sparkling (of seeds)

In the ashtray
(grey) cooled chilly
lumps of ash
yellowish-white crumpled
twisted (lined)
cigarette-end
trace of lips

in the ashtray
lumps of grey ash
extinguished (without light)
yellowish-white
a cigarette-end
crushed with a finger
trace of lips

in the ashtray
cooled lumps

of ash
a white cigarette-end
finger-crushed
trace of lipstick

jar full of jam
pink lump
with dark moist
interior
transparent edges
dark seeds
along the edges

moist sweet
lump in green jar
blobs of light
dark pale seeds

On a white
china plate
next to a pored lemon
an egg
two tomatoes covered
in taut red skin
on a white plate
a smooth (pale) egg
a lemon with a transparent interior
two red tomatoes

A glass drained of tea
in the glass a spoon
nickel-sheen
on the bottom of the glass
black tea-dregs

A glass
a metal spoon
moist brown
tea leaves

spectacle case
blue
pocket diary
white lettering
1970

A fly on a (match-)
box cleans
her transparent wings

grey-white
Chinese thermos strange signs
letters

a small still-life
contracts quietens
cures
sends to sleep

the fly regularly
hits the pane
the drip wears the stone

on a tin plate
mushrooms
brown warm hats
rough roots
sprinkled with earth

a small still-
life half in light
the other part in shadow

the fly hits the window
behind which stands
great mother nature
with a clump of trees
a road
and a postman

who is coming close
to me
(to the house)

EPILOGUE TO THE POEM

One must remove words
slowly carefully

peel image off image
colours off shapes
feelings off images
down to the core
to the language of suffering
till death

Some poems
are internal
some external
some poems are complete palpable
tossed
onto the surface
by knowledge routine
clear crystalline
radiant
like light
others are
fluid dreamlike
dark

1974

Autumnal

When it rains
I lie flat extended expansively far
in a mist

I feel stretched beneath the skin
moist twigs of blackthorn
prickly and dark

the hairy blood-vessels
of plant stems

blood flows upwards rust
bile verdigris
and colours the plain

on the rim
of the coal basin
a horse and plough
form a pastoral composition
extensive forgotten

Thorn

I don't believe
I don't believe from morning
till night

I don't believe from the one shore of my life
to the other
I don't believe
as patently deeply
as my mother
believed

I don't believe
when I eat bread
drink water
love a body

I don't believe
in his altars
symbols and priests

I don't believe
in the fields and the rain
in air
or the gold of annunciation

I read his parables
simple as an ear of corn
and think of the god
who did not laugh

I think of the small
god bleeding
amid white
sheets of childhood

or the thorn which tears

our eyes and lips
now
and in the hour of our death

The End

the beginning

a face
tightened
gnarled
convulsed

twisted into a single
coil
a knotted rope
or cord

slowly
it starts to unwind
loosen
fall
in the silence

it hung down

collapsed
and sagged

into fear humiliation
into the final defeat
into nothing

1968

Kazimierz Przerwa-Tetmajer

on 18 January 1940
in Nazi-occupied
Warsaw
they found
a homeless wretch
lying in the gutter
he died
without regaining consciousness

but this moment
has to be awaited
patiently and long
the monsters are still plunged
in sleep
in the brain

that drop of blood
pulsating
in the mysterious interior
of the future
the tissue
which will suffer degeneration

München 1899

Kazimierz Przerwa-Tetmajer
looks at Boecklin's
'Island of the Dead'
in the Neue Pinakotheke
people are sailing away like mists
from the meadow on to the lake They go to rest
another year
and it will be the 20th century

a son will be born

the firstborn
slayer of his father

a new growth

but for this we still have to wait

found in 1940
the unknown starveling
declaimed deliriously
mumbled

'upon a couch of soft white down
rayed by the glorious sun above
Danaë yearning for Zeus her love
from maiden limbs slips off her gown'

1967–68

Grass

I grow
in the bondings of walls
where they are
joined
there where they meet
there where they are vaulted

there I penetrate
a blind seed
scattered by the wind

patiently I spread
in the cracks of silence
I wait for the walls to fall
and return to earth

then I will cover
names and faces

1962

Re-education

the poet speaks
the same language to

a child
a provocateur
a priest
a politician
a policeman

the child smiles
the provocateur feels ridiculed
the politician slighted
the priest threatened
the policeman
buttons up his coat

the embarrassed poet
asks forgiveness
and repeats
his mistake

1969

Feeding Time

The city's
abdomen
covered with neons
emerges from
smoke and smog

and fades

whores
perform mechanical
movements
with a dead and distant look

voices
of copulating
grown-ups
frighten
children
on the other side of the screen

tiger the god clamped
in an iron cage
in the zoo
blinks his yellow eyes

it's not
feeding and opening time yet
tiger the god snoozes
amid his own
excrement

'a white night . . .'

a white night
dead light
rests on the linen

a white night
a spectre of night

during such nights
fruit does not fall
from trees

the poet has opened
the veins of verses

in such light
furniture stands
in a cold hell
stains grow
upon the floor

a white night
a dead body
lies on the table
blood-drained animal
upon an altar

behind the wall
a man and a woman

on the sheets blood
a facsimile of love

1969

'the reality . . .'

the reality
I had observed
through a smeared window
of a waiting room

I saw
face to face

weak
I turned away
from my weakness

I turned away
from illusions

upon the sands
of my words
someone drew the sign
of a fish
and walked away

1969

Regio

VESTIBULUM VAGINAE

in a dark warm
rough
elongating
cellar

strewn
with stifling damp
potatoes
rotted in springtime
sprouted
milky shoots
out of blind
little eyes

a smell
of decaying hay
sweet putrefaction

a place for
initiations
mysteries
enacted by children
the only heavenly dwellers
on earth

here
nature unveiled the mystery of sex
unveiled the womb
the rectum
sweetness welled
dark thick
warm

a cellar
here as innocent
as birds dogs
insects
we feverishly groped for
that suspected entrance
closed
by tight
lips

rima pudendi

imitating the observed
movements of animals
blinded by premonition
we crawled
out of the burrow into sunlight

the day caught us
into its clear eye
the vestibule
of the pouch
closed

TEMPLUM

The temple of the god of love
at Karakorum
stone tortoises
in the hour-glass of the desert
eight-armed
plump oval
smiling god
his caresses
are multiplied a hundredfold
the ecstatic faces
of mortal women
testify

further on
the same but in a different shape
he mounts a woman
like a steed
beastlike he
thrusts the seed into her

a soft green paradise
unfolds all round
further on
hands legs
thighs
upon shoulders
like white wings
raised above the head
where the earth is
there the sky in the whites of the eyes
reversed
turned over
in elongated
motionless eyes

impaled on his phallus
like a spit
open-mouthed
she embraces
and grips the god
with her lip

mortal

tied into a faceless knot
bodies
continue
to unite
standing
like naked columns

Beyond black silky waters
beneath the transparent surface
of paradise
the world of the damned
pants and burns

slim silver
bodies of women
glide
like leaves
fall into the flames
amid smiling lions
slit-eyed tigers
amid furry foxes and wolves
amid roses and birds of paradise
a forest of phalluses rises
to heaven

the moon and the sun roll radiant heads
along soft maidenly
slopes

VESTIBULUM VAGINAE—THE RETURN

ripening bodies
hid from
the threatening eye
of bearded god the father

in the dark
warm
elongating
cellar
sex organs
coupled in imagination
with the genitals
of animals insects and birds

with the ovules of plants

through the little window
smashed into light

before our eyes
butterflies coupled in mid-air
the witch toads in damp grass
there were noisy
dog weddings
a black stallion
reared
pranced
fell on the mare
his pliant phallus
darting like a flame
emerged from a black sheath
neighing filled the air

tiny trembling bodies shuddered
a livid flame
swayed above the ground

the image thundered
soared into the air
our lips were parched
burnt
our thighs pressed
the oval backs of galloping beasts

we groped for breath

LIPS MOUTHS

Huge heavy white
rounded heaving
breasts
of a stripper

inside black parted
fur
labia
majora
labia minora sweet life
regio
land region
frontier
heavenly ground
regio femoris
regio orbitalis
regio oralis
labial zone
in the labial zone
we distinguish labial red
rubor labiorum

OVUM

world egg
full of
light

we swarmed
like black sperm
battering
against an impenetrable
membrane

enclosed it sprouted
rainbowed
like a soap bubble
in which the sky
whirled

it was bursting under the strain
of our instincts
it opened

we penetrated
into a landscape
into human meat
into animal flesh
into colours
smells
lips were parting
revealing

a small
spark-like
devil
hopped into paradise

and bespectacled
stern god the father
said
betrachten Wir
unseren Leib
als Tempel Gottes
denn wir nicht entweihen
dürfen*

the egg of the world
closed

the seed was buried
nakedness hidden
the body grew
into pain
more and more acute

the modest lips
closed

* Let us consider our bodies to be like the temple of
God, which we must not profane.

MONS PUBIS

that night
war came near
to a seedy
night-spot
in the red district of a port

newspaper headlines grew
by the hour
orders had been issued
the ships of two superpowers
steamed head-on

Parisian strip-tease
a white face
in it carved
eyes and lips

in that room
a woman
gave herself
to all

newspaper headlines grew
the holocaust was at hand
mechanical music
blared
in a red light
a tall
blonde
was taking off
was parting
a transparent robe
her thighs gleamed with phosphorescent
light
she touched her lips
with her fingers
slowly parted

her lips
in a cloud of light
her hands rested
on her womb
she rolled her hands
from foot to throat
and across

she gave herself to herself
she gave herself to objects
to music
light
which fell on her
vertical red
blue gold
she encompassed
enclosed
enveloped
an invisible bird
a white swan

rubor labiorum

a stream of light
rushed upon her open face
into her mouth
it carried within it
all the men
gathered there

she rested her hands
on her mons veneris

when the men
the old and the young
in white shirts
ties
yawning with tension
glasses in hand

smiling
floated down
along her thin tapering fingers
rounded off
with ruby silver
little claws
to the vestibulum vaginae
the cloud of light
covered the woman
the labial redness split
sharp piercing
music
burst upon the silence

lights came on
the woman was moving away
parted her coat
for a second
weary smiling
her face between her legs
vanished behind a heavy curtain

1969

I Did Espy a Marvellous Monster

Dead alive
he still begets
gold

During the silly season
in the tabloids
Pablo Picasso
surfaces next to
the sea-serpent

A monster
from the prehistory
of art

he lived scavenged and jested
in the belly of the world
on market-days

A quarter of a century ago
he appeared in Kraków
on Karmelicka Street
precisely at noon

first a huge bald head
then burning black eyes
a highland jerkin on his back
a mountain axe in hand

passers-by surrounded him
onlookers who swarm
round an accident
or a beer-stall

a white dove
incredibly clean

and transparent flew out of
his sun-darkened hands

the showman
lived in several homes and castles
surrounded by dead quick wives
reproduced produced children pictures
a hundred
two hundred
three hundred
million dollars
in Pyskowice and Gliwice
house-painters took to
painting apartments à la pikaso
instead of 'stop being a Titian'
people now said 'stop this pikassing'

Then came the news
he'd died and his will
was being contested
the corpse stirred
pictures tumble down
from walls of private galleries
auction rooms museums chapels and banks

they rise in price

He—pregnant
an art necropolis
a rose of the winds
gives birth to gold coins
smiles at me
ironically and vanishes
round the corner into the cosmos
while I myself
27 years younger
walk
to Krupnicza Street

on the way I buy
tea sugar
rolls and smoked sausage

at home a task
awaits me:
To create poetry after Auschwitz

The Rose

It's only
an accidental
scratch

in sleep perhaps
on a journey
through carelessness

it's nothing
it doesn't hurt
now

red it opens
in the middle
of the night slowly
blossoms to the quick
of the meat of the word
carnivorous black
Isenheimer Altar
explosion of the sun
god
yellow Grünewald

in the hard practical
light
of day
the black iceberg of night flows away

and a fiery chariot
in a smoky sky

tipsy prostitutes
at the railway station
whisper lisp
master master

the mystic Rose
die mystische Rose
master master master
the smell of beer and urine
my time is up

'I yelled at Her . . .'

I yelled at Her
ten years ago

she went away
shod in shining
black paper

'don't make any excuses
—she said—
there's no need'

I yelled at Her
in an empty
hospital corridor

it was July a heatwave
the oil-paint on the walls
peeled

linden trees
scented the city park
covered in soot

godless
I wanted to weep for her
when dying and breathless
she was pushing back
empty and terrifying otherworlds
for a twinkling of an eye
she returned home into the country
in her last hour
I wanted to plead for her
a stretch of meadow
a tree
a cloud a bird

I see her tiny feet
in large paper coffin
slippers

I sat between
the table and the coffin
godless I willed a miracle
in an industrial panting
city in the second half
of the 20th century

dragged out of me into light
that thing
weeps

Descending

In memoriam Kazimierz Wyka

Now
descending
I look back
dawdling
I am like a man
who has lost something
but I'm not looking
around me

sometimes in the middle of the night
in myself or precisely at noon
in myself
I search and find
someone opens and shuts me
I look back
and move on

a green meadow

I stand open
in the light of day

1976

'That rustle . . .'

That rustle

life pouring
from a world full of objects
into death

it's through me
like a hole
in reality
this world pushes through
into the next

I think this through to the end
he whom
I sought above
waits below

in a burrow
a transfiguration

languid braying
of trumpets kneaded
out of waste-paper
rolled out of
newsprint

a rising from the dead
absentminded
futile

1976

'I was sitting in an easy-chair . . .'

I was sitting in an easy-chair
I stopped reading
suddenly I heard
my heart beating
it was so unexpected
as though a stranger had entered into me
and hammered with a clenched fist
some unknown creature
locked inside me
there was something indecent
in its battering with no relation
to me
to my abstract thought

1979

Picture

Who will recognize him

mother father brothers
that other woman perhaps
whose face
in a clouded mirror
flows down like rain

and you
when you look at yourself
what do you see

I see a man created
in the image and likeness of a god
who's gone

1979

'Doors in walls of houses . . .'

Doors in walls of houses
doors to kitchens doors to bedrooms
doors to lecture halls
and hotel rooms

one day
I saw a door
in a forest
beneath the door an ant-hill
a door in a garden
a door in a country lane
beyond the door a hare
a museum door
behind the door
'Stefan Batory at Pskov'

a door on the beach
beyond the door the sea
the closed door
of an airliner
behind the door the globe

the armour-plated door
of the Tower of London
behind the door a golden crown
a diamond the size
of a hen's egg
and Adam
smiling

1979

Photograph

today I received an old card
from a distant country
a picture of Erbalunga

I had never heard that name
I don't know where it is
and I don't wish to know

Erbalunga

yesterday I received
mother's photograph
saved from 1944

in the photograph
mother is still young beautiful
smiling faintly

but on the reverse
I read words written
in her own hand
'1944 terrible for me'

in 1944
the Gestapo
had murdered my elder brother

we hid his death
from mother
but she saw through us
and hid it
from us

1979

Tate Gallery Shop

A youth with the face of a saint
from a sweet Pre-Raphaelite picture
slowly descends to earth

another leaves the gents

misty blue eyes
a cross on a bared chest

patches on his knees
patches on his elbows
tiny hearts on his buttocks

an hour ago I had seen him
in a Soho pizzeria

multiplied by mirrors
in gilded art nouveau frames
absent
unconscious
he crossed the room
stopped
An Angel Standing in the Sun

I held my breath
hoping no one
would jostle him

meanwhile He combed his hair and beard
with his astral fingers
squinted
and postured
before the mirrors
he was turning into
a male prostitute

from the fiery furnace
from the juke-box
issued the voices of the innocents

The other stood
against a column
like a false St Sebastian
drank beer from a bottle

he moved
sauntered swayed
dragged his behind
carelessly
like a tart

a dirty pink comb
in the back pocket
of tightly-fitting trousers
the fingers of his other hand
stroked his genitals
as if he was checking
they hadn't dropped off

he foamed at the mouth
in his throat
inarticulate sounds
bubbled
spat out cores of words
which buzzed in their beards
like flies in a spider-web

a conversation of flowers

then they burst out
laughing
and spilled over

two carbuncles
open sores
out of a painting
by Francis Bacon

1975–81

Tree-Felling

In memory of Jarosław Iwaszkiewicz, author of 'Gardens'

A ceaseless anxiety
reigns among the crowns

a tree scored
for felling
with a white mark of annihilation
was still breathing
its boughs and branches
clawing
at the fleeting clouds

the leaves trembled and withered
sensing death

Trees don't move
from place to place
in search of nourishment
they can't escape
the saw
and the axe

a ceaseless anxiety
reigns among the crowns

tree-cutting is an execution
void of ceremony

spitting sawdust
the mechanical saw
enters the bark the pulp and the core
like lightning

struck at its side
it collapsed

and fell into the undergrowth
with its dead weight
it squashed grass and herbs
slender light blades
and trembling gossamer

together with the tree
they destroyed its shade
transparent
ambiguous
image
sign
appearing
in the light
of the sun and moon

The diligent roots
have yet no inkling
of the loss of the trunk
and crown

slowly
the surface death of the tree
reaches below ground

the roots of neighbouring trees
touch
enter into relationships
and bonds

beside men and beasts
the only living sentient beings
created in the image
and likeness of gods

Trees
cannot hide from us

Children born
painlessly in clinics
maturing
in discotheques
torn apart by artificial light
and sound
gaping at TV screens
do not converse
with trees

Trees of childhood cut burnt
poisoned dead
turn green over our heads
in May
shed leaves on graves
in November
grow within us
unto death

February 1981

Description of a Poem

I tried to remember
that ideal
unwritten
poem

nearly ripe
shaped in the night
tangible
it was sinking
and dissolving in the light of day
it did not
exist

at times I felt it
on the tip of the tongue
anxiously
I would sit down pen
in hand
waiting patiently
until convinced
it was an illusion
I would walk away

the poem was probably
a poem about itself
as a pearl
speaks of pearls
and a butterfly of butterflies

it was neither a love-poem
nor an elegy
it neither mourned
nor praised
it neither described
nor judged

that poem
which eludes me in daylight
has hidden itself in itself
only sometimes
I feel its bitterness
and internal warmth
but I don't pull it out of
the dark hollow depth
on to the flat bank
of reality

unborn
it fills the emptiness
of a disintegrating world
with unknown speech

1981

Works by Tadeusz Różewicz in English Translation

Faces of Anxiety, translated by Adam Czerniawski, London and Chicago, 1969

The Card-Index and Other Plays, translated by Adam Czerniawski, London and New York, 1969

The Witnesses and Other Plays, translated by Adam Czerniawski, London, 1970

The Survivor and Other Poems, translated by M. J. Krynski and R. A. Maguire, Princeton, 1976

Selected Poems, translated by Adam Czerniawski, Harmondsworth, 1976

Unease, translated by Victor Contoski, St Paul, Minnesota, 1980

Index of Titles